Palgrave Studies in Prisons and Penology

Edited by: **Ben Crewe**, University of Cambridge, Yvonne Jewkes, University of Leicester and Thomas Ugelvik, University of Oslo

This is a unique and innovative series, the first of its kind dedicated entirely to prison scholarship. At a historical point in which the prison population has reached an all-time high, the series seeks to analyse the form, nature and consequences of incarceration and related forms of punishment. *Palgrave Studies in Prisons and Penology* provides an important forum for burgeoning prison research across the world.

Series editors:

BEN CREWE is Deputy Director of the Prisons Research Centre at the Institute of Criminology, University of Cambridge, UK and co-author of *The Prisoner*.

YVONNE JEWKES is Professor of Criminology, Leicester University, UK. She has authored numerous books and articles on the subject and is editor of the *Handbook on Prisons*.

THOMAS UGELVIK is Senior Research Fellow in the Department of Criminology at the University of Oslo, Norway and editor of *Penal Exceptionalism? Nordic Prison Policy and Practise*.

Advisory Board:

Anna Eriksson, Monash University, Australia
Andrew M. Jefferson, Rehabilitation and Research Centre for Torture Victims, Denmark
Shadd Maruna, Queen's University Belfast, Northern Ireland
Jonathon Simon, UC Berkely, California, US
Michael Welch, Rutgers University, New Jersey, US

Titles include:

Vincenzo Ruggiero and Mick Ryan
PUNISHMENT IN EUROPE
A Critical Anatomy of Penal Systems

Phil Scraton and Linda Moore
THE INCARCERATION OF WOMEN
Punishing Bodies, Breaking Spirits

Peter Scharff Smith
WHEN THE INNOCENT ARE PUNISHED
The Children of Imprisoned Parents

Thomas Ugelvik
POWER AND RESISTANCE IN PRISON
Doing Time, Doing Freedom

Marguerite Schinkel
BEING IMPRISONED
Punishment, Adaptation and Desistance

Palgrave Studies in Prisons and Penology
Series Standing Order ISBN 978–1–137–27090–0 (hardback)

You can receive future titles in this series as they are published by placing a standing order. Please contact your bookseller or, in case of difficulty, write to us at the address below with your name and address, the title of the series and the ISBN quoted above.

Customer Services Department, Macmillan Distribution Ltd, Houndmills, Basingstoke, Hampshire RG21 6XS, England

Being Imprisoned

Punishment, Adaptation and Desistance

Marguerite Schinkel
Research Fellow, University of Glasgow, UK

First published 2014 by
PALGRAVE MACMILLAN

Palgrave Macmillan in the UK is an imprint of Macmillan Publishers Limited,
registered in England, company number 785998, of Houndmills, Basingstoke,
Hampshire RG21 6XS.

Palgrave Macmillan in the US is a division of St Martin's Press LLC,
175 Fifth Avenue, New York, NY 10010.

Palgrave Macmillan is the global academic imprint of the above companies
and has companies and representatives throughout the world.

Palgrave® and Macmillan® are registered trademarks in the United States,
the United Kingdom, Europe and other countries.

ISBN: 978–1–137–44082–2

This book is printed on paper suitable for recycling and made from fully
managed and sustained forest sources. Logging, pulping and manufacturing
processes are expected to conform to the environmental regulations of the
country of origin.

A catalogue record for this book is available from the British Library.

Library of Congress Cataloging-in-Publication Data

Schinkel, Marguerite, 1977–
    Being imprisoned : punishment, adaptation and desistance / Marguerite Schinkel
  Research Fellow, University of Glasgow, UK.
       pages cm.—(Palgrave studies in prisons and penology)
    ISBN 978–1–137–44082–2 (hardback)
    1. Imprisonment – Social aspects – Scotland. 2. Punishment – Scotland.
  3. Ex-convicts – Scotland – Attitudes. I. Title.
HV9649.S35S35 2014
365'.609411—dc23   2014021

Contents

Foreword
Fergus McNeill   vi

Acknowledgements   viii

Glossary   ix

1   Introduction   1

2   Meanings and Experiences of Punishment   13

3   Purposes Perceived in the Sentence   28

4   Legitimacy and the Impact of the Prison Environment   62

5   Narrative Demands and Desistance   95

6   Conclusion   119

Appendix I: Narrative Vignettes   135

Appendix II: Narrative Methods   146

Notes   161

Bibliography   163

Index   175

Foreword

Most researchers, quite sensibly, settle for a pathway that is well trodden even if it is not easy. They aim to apply their commitment and scholarly rigour to the challenge of making incremental advances in a given field of knowledge or in seeking better answers to fairly specific and narrow questions. Their work is important to the academy and to policy and practice. Usually, it deserves our attention and respect.

However, in my assessment, those who take the risks of asking new questions and/or of trying to establish new connections between different topics and questions deserve special admiration and attention. The risks they face are considerable. Firstly, they might fail to discover or to establish the connections they seek. Secondly, even if they succeed in doing so, colleagues used to asking the usual questions in the usual ways may find it hard to know where to place (dare I say pigeonhole?) the new contribution. Worse still, they may consciously or subconsciously resist the way in which the new contribution challenges the traditional approach to 'dividing and conquering' the subject.

In this important, compelling and challenging book, Marguerite Schinkel offers one such original and challenging contribution to contemporary criminology. This is not an 'effects of imprisonment' book. It is not a 'philosophy of punishment' book. It is not a 'desistance' book or a 'reentry' book. Rather, it is a book in which she connects these related and yet rarely connected literatures. Moreover, it explores how these themes are connected not just conceptually but also *empirically* in the narratives of long-term prisoners during and after imprisonment. As its title suggests, this book examines what *Being Imprisoned* means to these men, not only as a lived *experience* but also as a *sanction*, thus connecting the realities of imprisonment with its perceived purposes, justice and legitimacy. That might have been an original enough contribution, but *Being Imprisoned* goes a step further, examining how the experience and the sanction of imprisonment *impact*, for better or worse, on life after imprisonment and on desistance from crime.

The author's ambition to and the book's success in connecting these concerns and questions is what should mark its original and significant contribution, not just to theory and research about punishment, imprisonment and desistance, but to addressing numerous related policy and practice challenges. For me, the central message of the book is that, in many ways, experiences and meanings of punishment and imprison-ment (and release) are profoundly incoherent and inconsistent. It is very hard to make sense of being imprisoned. We might infer that this is one of the reasons for the ineffectiveness of imprisonment, at least in securing rehabilitation. But it is only by taking the risk of connecting different fields of scholarship that *Being Imprisoned* allows us to see this incoherence and inconsistency in sharper focus.

If we are prepared to match Marguerite Schinkel's courage and ambi-tion, then we will have work to do in thinking much more carefully about how to resolve or address the incoherence and inconsistency of contemporary punishment. Helpfully, the concluding chapter offers several thoughtful and helpful suggestions about how we might begin to do so. But *Being Imprisoned* will have achieved more than many other worthy criminological works, not just if its conclusions are accepted and recommendations are followed, but if it inspires its readers to rise to the challenge of thinking afresh about the coherence of punishment for themselves.

Fergus McNeill
University of Glasgow
April 2014

Acknowledgements

Sitting on an airplane, flying home, is an interesting time to take stock. Underslept, underfed, and despite that literally above it all, I realise there are many people on the ground below to whom I owe thanks.

I would like to thank, first and foremost, the interviewees who shared their thoughts with me. I hope I've done your stories justice.

This book would not exist, and I would not be where I am now, if it wasn't for Fergus McNeill. From the very first 'delighted' email he sent me about this research, to the perfect Viva card, his enthusiasm and positive attitude have sustained me throughout this project. His insights have also on many occasions re-inspired me and allowed me to see my data in a new light. Thank you for your intellectual and academic generosity. Thanks to Richard Sparks, who went above and beyond the expected. I have missed our meetings, which always led to new ideas and renewed motivation. Thanks also to Antony Duff, whose module on Crime and Punishment kindled an interest in how (and if) we should punish that still has me gripped. His work, with its searching analysis of what lies behind the taken-for-granted, impressed (and continues to impress) me deeply.

I would like to thank Julia Willan and Harriet Barker at Palgrave for their enthusiasm, patience and promptness in answering my questions and the guidance they provided. The research that the book is based on was made possible by funding from the Economic and Social Research Council and support from the Scottish Prison Service and the Association of Directors of Social Work. I am particularly grateful to Dan Gunn, for opening up possibilities in more than one establishment.

Closer to home, thanks to Merlin, for all our adventures together. I am looking forward to new ones, as always. And thanks to Tomlin for the looks, laughs and topsy-turvy ideas that brighten up my days. Yes, yes for the yes indeed. With both of you, I am the lucky one.

Last, but certainly not least, I am grateful to my parents, Henk and Sytske, for allowing me to go my own way, dream my own dreams and take my own pace. Your support for me as a care worker, student and researcher has given me the time and space to meander my way to this project. Gratitude is also due to Aag and Frans, who have helped me build my academic confidence with their unfailing interest. Having such a dedicated first audience has made all the difference.

Glossary

brew	unemployment benefit (or the agency that administers it)
digger	segregation unit
done	attacked/hurt
doubled up	made to share a cell
gutted	very upset/devastated
ICM meeting	Integrated Case Management meeting – representatives from the prison and outside agencies meet with the prisoner present to put plans into place to reduce reoffending upon release
ken	know/you know
lib	liberate/release
mug	fool
peter	cell
wean	child
wee	small/little

1
Introduction

Introduction

Criminal punishment represents the state's most serious intrusion upon the human rights of its citizens. However, beyond (ex-)offender autobiographies, there is remarkably little in-depth empirical evidence about how those who are punished interpret their sentence. This book starts to address this gap in our knowledge – based on narrative interviews with 27 (ex-)prisoners in Scotland, it explores how these men saw their sentence, its impact and their future.

There is an increasing criminological literature on the criminal careers of offenders, including how they come to desist from crime (Giordano, Cernkovich and Rudolph, 2002; Maruna, 2001; Sampson and Laub, 2003) and a well-developed body of work on the lived experience of the conditions of imprisonment (Carrabine, 2004; Crewe, 2009; Liebling, 2004; Sparks, Bottoms and Hay, 1996; Sykes, 1958). Some of this work has touched on the ways in which punishment is given meaning. For example, Crewe (2009) found that only a limited number of prisoners opposed their sentence and both Sampson and Laub (2003) and Giordano et al. (2002) noted that some people saw their prison sentence as a turning point in their lives. However, so far the question of how criminal punishment is interpreted has received little detailed attention (Rex, 2005). Moreover, criminological research has provided limited knowledge of which aspects of imprisonment (if any) help people to deal with problems both before and after release. Yet, long-term imprisonment is the most serious sentence available in most Western jurisdictions, and a very costly one at that, with the annual average cost per prisoner in Scotland being £32,146 (Scottish Prison Service, 2012). If the process by which imprisonment is given meaning

1

and is evaluated in terms of fairness has the power to contribute in any way to desistance and reintegration (positively or negatively), then it is imperative that we know more about this process and the factors that influence it.

This book examines the narratives of long-term prisoners, with a special focus on the meaning they ascribe to their sentence, and the consequences of this for their future offending. As the title suggests, it is about how prisoners make sense of 'being imprisoned', and the personal and practical consequences of this process of meaning-making for their present and future lives. The book thereby aims to bring together strands of literature that have so far remained mostly separate: the literature on prison life and the moral performance of prisons; the literature on desistance; and the more theoretical literature on the purposes and legitimacy of criminal punishment.

With this in mind, the purpose of this book is two-fold. First of all, it aims to give a fine-grained account of the way in which long-term prisoners give meaning to their sentence. This is intended to start addressing the gap in the literature about how sentences are experienced *as a sanction* by those who undergo them. As noted above, there is a well-developed literature on the experience of imprisonment, but this tends to focus on matters internal to the prison, thereby failing to connect this experience to issues of justice and the lives within which prisoners give their sentence meaning. By providing a more contextual account it becomes possible to connect in-prison experiences with pre- and (projected) post-prison biographies, leading to a deeper understanding of the impact of sentences and the way in which their meaning is dependent on what has come before and follows after.

Furthermore, a more in-depth and contextual account of the experience of imprisonment allows for an exploration of how it connects (or fails to do so) with processes of desistance. So far, most studies of desistance have focused on studying desistance *per se*, examining the processes that help people to desist (for example Maruna, 2001). In doing so, some studies have found that criminal punishment, and especially imprisonment, *can* be experienced as helpful in moving away from crime (for example Aresti, 2010; Giordano et al., 2002). On the other hand, the criminogenic effects of imprisonment have been well documented (Liebling and Maruna, 2005). With increasing pressure (and with the aspiration in many jurisdictions) to make sentences effective, and with imprisonment as the punishment of choice for the most serious and troublesome offenders, an examination of how imprisonment and desistance interact is essential. The extent to which a sentence facilitates desistance will depend on how it is perceived and given meaning. At the most basic level, if the punishment is experienced as unjust, this is more likely to lead to a negative view of the authorities, reduced motivation to abide by the rules (Franke, Bierie and Mackenzie, 2010; Robinson and McNeill, 2008) and ultimately, to future offending (Sherman, 1993), rather than to desistance. More specifically, Maruna (2001) has pointed out that the pressure to take responsibility for the crime committed that is exerted in most sentences may be counter-productive for the subjective meaning-making processes that support desistance, including seeing oneself as essentially good. How a sentence fits in with one's wider life is likely to have an impact on desistance: how much one loses through imprisonment (in terms of housing, jobs, relationships, but also self-respect), and what resources are still in place to counteract these deprivations, will influence whether desistance is more or less likely after imprisonment.

The second purpose of the book is to provide an empirical examination of the most commonly used justifications of punishment. Because criminal punishment in general, and (long-term) imprisonment in particular (Carrabine, 2004; Mathiesen, 1965; Sparks et al., 1996; Sykes, 1958) is a serious intrusion by the state into private lives, it is important to examine whether it achieves its stated aims. Only by examining lived experience is it possible to see whether the justifications given for punishment fit the ways it plays out in the lives and minds of the punished. Usually states, their institutions and employees use a mix of rationales when justifying punishment. On the one hand, they tend to justify punishment through its positive effect of reducing crime (and in current idiom thereby 'protecting the public'). Deterrence, rehabilitation, reform and incapacitation are all often cited as the aims (and justifications) of punishment. On the other hand, they also justify criminal justice practice in more retributive terms, relying on the idea that there is an intrinsic link between crime and punishment, and that the sentence is the offender's 'just deserts'. For example, the most recent Scottish specification of the purpose of sentences was given in the Criminal Justice and Licensing (Scotland) Bill of 2010. It stated that sentences should aim to achieve:

> the punishment of offenders, the reduction of crime (including its reduction by deterrence), the reform and rehabilitation of offenders, the protection of the public, and the making of reparation by offenders to persons affected by their offences. (Section 1.1)

As is common in many jurisdictions, the Bill expresses mixed purposes for sentencing related to crime reduction (deterrence, reform and rehabilitation) and retributive punishment.

Few of these purposes of sentencing can be seen as achieved if they are not reflected in the experiences of the punished. Deterrence depends on people being aware of the threat of punishments, finding these punishments sufficiently aversive and thinking they are likely enough to get caught to refrain from offending (in the future). Reform and rehabilitation require that people think, or at least act, differently than before in relation to offending. The retributive insistency on 'just deserts' makes the experiences of the punished relevant to punitive purposes as well. Because offences have to be punished proportionally (the more serious crimes should be punished more severely) it is necessary to know how much suffering each punishment imposes. In reality, the assumption is made that the 'same' punishment, say four years in prison, affects everyone in the same way, but some have argued that an effort should be made to anticipate the actual experience of suffering for each individual (Curran, MacQueen and Whyte, 2007; Kolber, 2009). Their reliance on suffering also means that retributive justifications depend on the adverse experience of punishment in a more fundamental way: if offenders actually experience their sentence as preferable to their usual life, then it does not fulfil its punitive function. Among the most commonly used justifications of punishment, only incapacitation could be said to work independently of people's internal worlds, because it controls their external one, although research by Wood et al. (2010) suggests that even this is only partially true.

With justifications of punishment generally focusing on the sentence itself, it is also important to examine whether the borders of the punishment lie where intended. Many believe that the only punishing aspect of imprisonment should be that it takes away prisoners' liberty (see for example Liebling, 2004, p. 305). However, it is well known that imprisonment has additional adverse consequences for many prisoners, in their personal and working lives, and long after they have been released. The stigma of imprisonment makes it more difficult to find employment (Pager, 2003; Schneider and McKim, 2003; Social Exclusion Unit, 2002). Imprisonment can have long-term negative health consequences (Massoglia, 2008; Schnittker and John, 2007) and released prisoners are at much higher risk of dying during their first two weeks of freedom, notably because the risk of a drug overdose is high (Binswanger et al., 2007; Bird and Hutchinson, 2003). Being imprisoned makes divorce more likely (Apel, Blokland, Nieuwbeerta and van Schellen, 2010) and has further negative consequences for the partners and children of prisoners, such as stigma, mental health problems, financial strain, (future) unemployment and an increased likelihood of drug use or involvement in criminal activity (Murray and Farrington, 2008; Murray, 2005, 2007). All in all, imprisonment places a burden on the prisoner (and his or her family) that extends far beyond (the period of) loss of liberty (Ewald and Uggen, 2012; Liebling and Maruna, 2005; Petersilia, 2000). This book therefore also examines what exactly long-term imprisonment encompasses in the eyes of those who experience it, and how this affects the sentence's legitimacy in their eyes.

Studying the meaning of imprisonment

The research that forms the basis for this book focused on the experiences of long-term prisoners, not explicitly excluding or including those given a life sentence. This population was chosen as being of special interest, because long-term prison sentences are the most intrusive sentence in their impact, taking away freedom and normality for a significant portion of a person's life. Long-term prisoners were also anticipated to be more likely than short-term prisoners to have reflected on their sentence and to have experience of a wider variety of aspects of sentencing. For example, whereas short-term imprisonment has relatively recently been described as mere warehousing (Scottish Prisons Commission, 2008), long-term prisoners in many jurisdictions usually have the opportunity to engage in work, education and programmes related to their offending. They also often receive some form of statutory post-release supervision and support once released on licence, which means that they will meet regularly with a probation or parole officer or (in Scotland) a criminal justice social worker in the community. Men and women were anticipated to make sense of their sentences in different ways, considering that among female prisoners substance abuse and mental health issues are even more prevalent than among male prisoners, and that they are more likely to be the main caregiver for their children (Commission on Women Offenders, 2012; HM Inspectorate of Prisons, 2010). With adult male offenders the most numerous and with obtaining access to multiple prisons problematic, it was decided to focus on this group. To explore the issues outlined in the rationale above, the following research questions were formulated:

- What meanings do prisoners give to their sentences? Do any of these meanings align with normative theories? How are these meanings ascribed?

- Do prisoners' accounts indicate that any of the stated aims of punishment are achieved?
- What unintended meanings and consequences do long-term prison sentences have?
- Do prisoners see their sentences as justified? Why (not)? What are the implications of this?
- Does the way prisoners see their sentence change as they progress through their sentence?

These questions were explored in twenty-seven interviews with three groups of long-term adult male prisoners: men at the start of their sentence, men at the end of their sentence and men on licence. This cross-sectional design was chosen to answer the question of how meanings change over time. A longitudinal design would have been ideal, with the same prisoners interviewed repeatedly, but given the time limits on the duration of the study and the length of the sentences imposed, this was impossible. Table 1.1 gives some basic information about each of the men, along with the pseudonyms they chose, which will be used in the remainder of this book. More in-depth information about their circumstances is contained in Appendix I, where the narratives that this book draws on most heavily are summarised.

The interviews were conducted in 2009 and 2010 in two prisons and two criminal justice social work offices in Scotland. Most interviews lasted between one and one and a half hours, with the shortest interview 39 minutes and the longest two hours and 20 minutes. Because the meanings of sentences ascribed by the punished have been studied so little, there was a strong possibility that the research questions would not capture all that was relevant. For this reason, and to answer the question of how meanings are ascribed in the context of people's lives, a narrative methodology was decided upon (see Appendix II for more details). As Polkinghorne writes:

> The storied descriptions people give about the meaning they attribute to life events is...the best evidence available to researchers about the realm of people's experience. (2007, p. 479)

While the interviews were mainly narrative, and explored the way the men interpreted their sentence and incorporated it in their wider life story, if they did not touch on questions of legitimacy and purpose spontaneously they were asked semi-structured questions about these issues at the end of the interview.

Table 1.1 Participants' characteristics

Pseudonym	Age	History	Offence type	Sentence
Participants at **start of sentence**				
Alan	40s	Previous short-term sentence	Drugs	4–5 years
Chris	40s	Previous short-term sentences	Drugs	4–5 years
David	35–39	No previous convictions	Driving	6–7 years
Malcolm	30–34	Previous long-term sentence	Drugs	6–7 years
Paul	40s	No previous convictions	Driving	6–7 years
Walter	30–34	Previous short-term sentences	Threats	4–5 years
Participants at **end of sentence**				
Alex	35–39	Previous long-term sentence	Violence	10 years
Colin	30–34	Previous short-term sentences	Drugs	4–5 years
Dan	60s	Previous long-term sentences	Violence	5–6 years + ext*
Devan	20–24	No previous convictions	Drugs	7–8 years
Doug	25–29	Previous short-term sentences	Violence	4–5 years + ext*
Gordon	20–24	No previous imprisonment	Violence	4–5 years
Graham	30–34	Previous short-term sentences	Violence	4–5 years
Ian	30–34	Previous long-term sentences	Theft	7–8 years + ext*
James	35–39	Previous long-term sentences	Drugs + violence	10 years
Neil	40s	Previous long-term sentence	Drugs	10 years
Peter	20–24	Previous short-term sentences	Violence	10 years
Robert	60s	Previous short-term sentence	Drugs	4–5 years
Participants on **licence**				
Andy	25–29	Previous short-term sentences	Violence	4–5 years
Jack	40s	Previous long-term sentence	Robbery	8–9 years
Lino	35–39	Previous long-term sentences	Weapon	4–5 years
Mark	35–39	Previous short-term sentences	Violence	5–6 years
Mohammed	30–34	Previous long-term sentence	Violence	8–9 years

continued

Table 1.1 Continued

Pseudonym	Age	History	Offence type	Sentence
Smitty	25–29	Previous short-term sentences	Drugs + driving	5–6 years
Stephen	50s	Previous long-term sentence	Violence	4–5 years
Tim	25–29	No previous imprisonment	Murder	Life
Tony	50s	Previous long-term sentences	Robbery	10+ years

* + ext = plus extended licence: a licence period beyond the end of the sentence was imposed.

In transcribing the interviews, the following notation, adapted from Banister et al. (1994) was used:

(.)	pause
(xxxx)	unintelligible speech
(judge)	doubtful transcription (best guess)
[laughs]	non-verbal utterances
[town]	substituting generic labels for specific names, to safeguard anonymity
/	overlapping speech or aborted statements
UPPER CASE	emphasis in speech

In addition, in the quotes in this book, occasionally ... is used to indicate where some speech or text has been omitted.

In this book, the accounts of the men at the end of their sentence and on licence are discussed in most depth, and are explicitly compared in Chapters 4 and 5. The men at the start of their sentence are not considered as a separate group. Chris, Malcolm and Walter had been imprisoned repeatedly before, and were very like those at the end of their sentence in their attitude towards imprisonment. David and Paul had been imprisoned for their first ever offence, both for death by dangerous driving, and accepted their sentence as justified because of the harm caused. The remaining interviewee, Alan, opposed his sentence. Therefore, this group was too small and disparate to form a separate basis for analysis.

The context of the study

Scotland, while part of the United Kingdom, has its own legal and criminal justice system, distinct from that in England and Wales. The imprisonment rate in Scotland (154 per 100,000 in 2011 (Scottish Government, 2012a)) is higher than for most other Western European countries, and has increased by more than 30 per cent since 1999–2000 (Scottish Government, 2009), despite a decrease in crime in the same period (Scottish Prisons Commission, 2008). Recently there has been political will to tackle the high rates of imprisonment, which an independent report commissioned by the government has acknowledged constitutes the warehousing of 'the damaged and traumatised' (Scottish Prisons Commission, 2008, p. 13). In February 2011 the Criminal Justice and Licensing (Scotland) Act 2010 came into effect. It includes a presumption against prison sentences shorter than three months. Despite the Criminal Justice and Licensing (Scotland) Bill, which this Act was based on, including the overarching statement of the purposes of sentencing discussed above, this section was removed under Amendment 38 (Munro, 2010) before the Bill was enacted, leaving overarching purposes of sentencing unspecified at the national level.

In contrast, the Scottish Prison Service revealed its new vision in November 2013, broadcasting a new, more rehabilitative direction. Whereas at the time the research interviews took place its official 'vision' was 'Making Scotland safer by protecting the public and reducing reoffending' (Scottish Prison Service, 2011), its new vision is 'Helping to Build a Safer Scotland – Unlocking Potential – Transforming Lives' (Scottish Prison Service, 2013, p. 2). In his speech announcing the change of direction, the Chief Executive of the Scottish Prison Service said:

> We have to be an organisation that believes within the heart of everyone associated with it that we are agents of hope and positive change. That everyone who passes through our care has the capacity and the ambition to succeed and that by doing so, can turn away from a destructive life of crime to become a valuable and contributive citizen. (McConnell, 2013)

He also promised individualised services, for prisoners, their families and their communities, meaning that some of the findings in Chapter 3 will hopefully become outdated if this vision is turned into reality.

In 2010 to 2011 there were 2,268 long-term adult prisoners in Scotland (Berman, 2012), who made up almost 30 per cent of the average daily prison population in 2011–2012 (Scottish Government, 2012a). Long-term imprisonment in Scotland is defined as imprisonment of four years or longer, and for the purposes of this book includes life sentence prisoners, one of whom was interviewed on licence. This is slightly shorter than the five years or longer used by the Council of Europe in its recommendations on long-term sentences (Council of Europe, 2003). Both these definitions of long-term sentences pale in comparison to what would be considered a long-term sentence in the United States. As far back as 1995 one US commentator noted that a sentence would have to be at least eight years long to be considered long-term in the US (Flanagan, 1995), and since then sentence lengths have increased substantially (Pew Center on the States, 2012). However, even though (much) longer sentences will have different meanings in prisoners' minds and lives than those discussed in this book, the factors in meaning-making reported here (such as finding a way to cope with the prison environment, institutionalisation and difficulties with reintegration) are likely to have even greater force for those serving longer sentences, and therefore will be relevant in other national contexts where much longer sentences are common.

In Scotland, those who are subject to long-term sentences are usually housed in different units and/or prisons from the short-term population and tend to have more access to work and educational activities (Scottish Prisons Commission, 2008). While short-term prisoners are released automatically after serving half of their sentence, for long-term prisoners this is the *earliest* possible release date, when the Parole Board makes a binding recommendation to Scottish Ministers on whether the prisoner should be released on parole. Thereafter, the Parole Board reconsiders the case every 16 months, until the prisoner has served two thirds of their sentence, at which point they are automatically released on licence. For the remainder of their sentence, they are supervised in the community by a criminal justice social worker.

The conditions and safety in prisons in Scotland has improved significantly over the past decade, and the way prisoners are treated by staff has been transformed over the last 30 years to the extent that now only three per cent of prisoners rate their relationships with staff negatively (HM Chief Inspector of Prisons for Scotland, 2009). The prison in which the interviews with men at the end of their sentence took place was particularly praised for its positive relationships between staff members and prisoners in a recent inspection report, which also noted that there was little violence between prisoners.

High levels of imprisonment have, along with other social problems, been linked to the level of inequality in a society (Wilkinson and Pickett, 2010). The Gini coefficient is one of the measures used to indicate inequality, with 0 representing perfect equality (where all the wealth is shared equally amongst people), and 100 representing perfect inequality (where one person holds all the wealth). Scotland's Gini coefficient in 2010–2011 was 30, compared to 34 for Great Britain as a whole (Scottish Government, 2012b). When looking at European figures from 2010, this places Scotland at about the average for European countries, with most Southern European and former Soviet Bloc countries showing higher levels and most Northern and Eastern European countries lower levels of inequality.[1] Within Scotland, it is the most deprived areas in which most police recorded crime takes place (Mooney, Croall and Munro, 2010). Research has also shown a linear correlation between the level of deprivation in neighbourhoods and the number of their residents in prison (Houchin, 2005), indicating that the most disadvantaged are imprisoned disproportionately. The interviews with men on licence took place in communities with income deprivation levels of almost 25 per cent (compared to 16 per cent nationally) and employment deprivation levels amongst those of working age of almost 20 per cent (compared to 13 per cent nationally), which placed them amongst the 15 per cent most deprived areas in Scotland.[2]

The structure of the book

This chapter has described the rationale and context for the research and has set out the questions that will be addressed in the book. Chapter 2 provides an overview of the literature on the purpose and fairness of sentences, as perceived by the punished, with a special focus on (long-term) imprisonment. The remainder of the book contains the research findings. Chapter 3 discusses what purposes were most salient in the interviewees' accounts, with a focus on reform, rehabilitation and deterrence. Here, the focus is very much on 'etic' level analysis, which uses concepts that originate elsewhere (Silverman, 2001); in this case the justifications of punishment most often used in policy and practice documents. The purpose of this chapter is to explore whether the meanings ascribed by prisoners to their sentence align with the stated aims of punishment and whether their accounts suggest that these aims are achieved. As the book progresses, the focus moves to analysis that is more grounded in the accounts of the men who were interviewed, and thus to a more 'emic' analysis of the meanings of imprisonment. This level of analysis employs the language used by the interviewees themselves and highlights concepts that would be meaningful to them – they come from 'inside' the research (Silverman, 2001). Chapter 4 focuses on perceptions of fairness. It argues that the prison environment made it difficult for many of the interviewees to oppose their sentence, leading instead to a form of acquiescence that was often presented as endorsement of the sentence's legitimacy. Chapter 5 examines the impact of the need to make sense of the prison sentence in the context of wider lives. It shows how the need for a positive narrative led some of the men to embrace their sentence (at least in hindsight) as a fulcrum for change and the catalyst of their transformation. In both these chapters I also consider the differences between the accounts of the men on licence and those coming to the end of their prison sentence. The concluding chapter, Chapter 6, draws the findings together, considers their limitations and significance beyond the research setting and discusses implications for policy and practice.

2
Meanings and Experiences of Punishment

Introduction

Many authors have recognised the importance of examining the views of offenders of the criminal justice process. Rex (2005) has argued for the need to see how well their views accord with justifications of punishment. Others have written that soliciting offenders' accounts is necessary in order to describe the system accurately, examine and possibly change it (Casper, 1972); to promote respect for the system (McGinnis and Carlson, 1981) because disrespect for the system may lead to further crime (Alpert and Hicks, 1977; Krohn and Stratton, 1980); and to make desistance or rehabilitation more likely (Larson and Berg, 1989). This chapter discusses what is already known about offenders' perceptions and experiences of their punishments, and further justifies the research focus by pointing out limitations of the existing research and gaps in the literature.

Perceptions of purpose

In order to explore how the punished make sense of their sentence and whether their views reflect the stated justifications of the punishment, it is important to examine what purposes of sentences they support and see as achieved. Several studies have surveyed those undergoing a sentence for their opinions on its purpose. For example, Patrick and Marsh (2001) surveyed 80 prisoners to find out whether they saw their sentence as aimed at rehabilitation or punishment and found that the majority of prisoners experienced their sentence as punitive. They report that prisoners were more likely to see prison as rehabilitative when they respected other prisoners and saw prison staff–prisoner relationships as positive and marked by cooperation rather than conflict. Rex (2005) surveyed 143 people serving community sentences, who felt that rehabilitation should be the main aim of criminal justice, followed by incapacitation, education and reform. However, even the least popular aim of sentencing on the questionnaire (retribution) was still supported by 40 per cent of offenders, compared to 79 per cent supporting rehabilitation, indicating that the differences in support for the 13 aims mentioned were relatively small. The main perceived purposes of imprisonment were retribution and deterrence. The participants generally supported reformative aims, followed by other aims that involved reducing offending, with the least support for moralising and exacting recompense for their crimes.

In another study of those serving community sentences, Applegate et al. (2009) surveyed 369 probationers in England. They found that more than 90 per cent felt that their order had deterred them from future crime, over 60 per cent felt probation was rehabilitative and over half thought it made them pay back for their crime. Just under half felt they deserved to be on probation. However, these seemingly high levels of support for different functions of probation are contradicted by the same study's results showing that over half of the participants felt that there was no purpose to being on probation and 44 per cent responded that probation did not help them or society in any way. This highlights a problem with the use of surveys to investigate attitudes. In all three of these studies, participants were asked to agree or disagree with statements reflecting possible purposes of their sentence. While participants were able to say whether they thought their sentence did or should achieve this aim, it is neither clear whether they would have thought of these aims independently nor whether any of these aims played an important role in the participants' own sense-making of their sentence.

In-depth qualitative studies are needed to overcome these limitations, but such studies rarely focus on questions of purpose, though there are a few exceptions. A recent Australian study investigated the meaning young men ascribed to their incarceration through narrative interviews (Halsey, 2007). The participants recounted that they thought the *intended* purposes of their incarceration were deterrence and rehabilitation. However, they did not feel that it achieved these aims because the environment was counterproductive. Deterrence was not achieved because the environment was familiar and not aversive for those in a young offenders' institute, where many described activities on offer that they could not access elsewhere. Its conditions were even experienced by some as providing a degree of respite from a more difficult life on the outside. Those interviewed in an adult prison did experience their incarceration as deprivation, because there was so little on offer, and many of them regretted not having changed their lives around in time to avoid this experience. The participants felt that they were not rehabilitated in the course of their confinement, because rehabilitative programmes were seen as inauthentic: they failed to match the participants' realities and were delivered by professionals who were seen as having no real understanding of the problems faced by offenders. Finally, the fact that the young people interviewed felt that authority in the prison was exercised inconsistently and without respect for prisoners led the author to write:

> if incarceration is designed to 'teach young men a lesson', then the curriculum, to continue the metaphor, is presently structured and relayed in a manner which elicits an abiding disrespect for and loss of faith in experts, authority, and so-called rehabilitative processes. (Halsey, 2007, p. 359)

With custody mostly seen as respite or as counterproductive by the participants, these findings suggest that for them imprisonment did not have much meaning, nor did it manage to fulfil the purposes by which it is often justified.

Another qualitative study focused exclusively on how the *punitive* purpose of imprisonment was reflected in offenders' accounts. Sexton (2007) interviewed 40 men and 40 women incarcerated in the US, many of whom were serving very long sentences (the average minimum sentence length was 19 years). Most of the respondents did not mention punishment spontaneously when describing their experiences in prison, but when asked about this aspect of their sentence specifically, they reported seeing their imprisonment as essentially punitive. This again illustrates that respondents will endorse (and are able to expand on) aspects of their sentence that are not necessarily of greatest importance to them. Sexton found that the two defining factors in experiences of punishment were salience and severity. Salience was determined by the way in which the participants' (current) experience of punishment compared to their expectations. If conditions were seen as less negative than expected, the salience of its punitive function was low and vice versa. The severity of the sentence was determined by whether people were prone to perceiving concrete punishments as symbolic (for example poor medical care as an indication that prison staff did not care whether they lived or died) and by the unit in which people were held. Housing units that attenuated the harshness of the prison environment through allowing some personal choice and the provision of laundry facilities, pool tables and a microwave were generally perceived as less severe than more traditional housing units. This fine-grained examination of the experience of punishment illuminates how the physical and relational conditions of the immediate living environment, and the way they are situated in relation to previous experiences, affect the experience of imprisonment.

Other work has highlighted that factors beyond the formal punishment and its conditions can also shape people's perceptions. Comfort (2008) interviewed ten heterosexual couples, in which the men had recently been released from prison. She found that some of her interviewees described their experiences as rehabilitative, despite a lack of useful programmes or other interventions offered by the prison regime. She writes:

> finding deliverance in merely having time to think quietly about one's life, deciding to adhere to a certain code of masculinity, and articulating that decision to loved ones opens the potential for betterment to virtually all inmates, paradoxically leading them to cast an environment barren of social welfare services as fertile ground for redemption. (p. 272)

Because sentences happen in the context of wider lives, factors beyond the prison regime and the criminal justice system can have a crucial impact on how sentences are perceived. Similar findings were reported by a phenomenological study of the experiences of 16 incarcerated young offenders. Despite generally adverse conditions, including bullying and a lack of rehabilitation work, most thought that they had changed for the better because they had had time to think or because they had not been able to use drugs (Ashkar and Kenny, 2008). This perception of rehabilitation existed in conjunction with their view that they had been deterred by the adverse experience of imprisonment. Conversely, in Presser's (2008) narrative study of 27 violent offenders, many 'criticized the rhetoric of treatment, which they said contrasted with a reality of actually facilitating recidivism' (p. 119). Again, the meaning ascribed to sentences may be very different from the stated intent or conditions of imprisonment.

A final study examined the aftermath of long-term imprisonment, and the perceived purpose of supervision after release. Appleton (2010) interviewed 28 men on life licence, who at the time of interview had been free for 8–13 years. She found that her participants generally saw

the supervision they received as care, with their probation officers genuinely interested in helping them, or as a benevolent mixture of care and
control, with only a minority feeling that their supervision was overly
focused on control. They therefore perceived their supervision as rehabilitative rather than punitive.

Perceptions of fairness

In order to connect prisoners' narratives with issues of justice, one of
this study's main research questions was whether (and why) the participants thought their sentence was fair. Leaving aside the literature on
procedural justice (see below), studies directly examining offenders'
perceptions of the fairness of their sentence are even scarcer than those
focusing on questions of purpose. An important early contribution was
made by Casper in 1972. He interviewed 71 men about their views of
the different stages of the criminal justice process, including arrest,
plea-bargaining, interactions with the attorney, prosecutors and judge,
and of the law in general. His findings were mostly negative. Casper
writes that, while the criminal justice system *should* teach the offender
moral lessons, the system was perceived by his interviewees as an
extension of life on the street, with the police, prosecution and public
defenders seen as driven by a 'production ethic'; merely doing their
jobs and trying to dispose of cases as quickly and easily as possible,
while pursuing their own interests. The judge was not perceived as
an impartial figure who cared about offenders' circumstances and
delivering justice, but as a largely irrelevant figurehead who merely
accepted the recommendations made by the prosecutor. In order to
secure the best possible outcome defendants felt they had to bargain,
manipulate the situation as best they could and have luck on their
side, which mirrored their experience of life outside. The police were
perceived as adversaries in a game, with defendants' reporting feelings of pride and satisfaction if they outwitted them. On the other
hand, when the defendants were not guilty of the particular crime for
which they were arrested, they referred to their 'general guilt', the fact
that they *had* committed similar crimes in the past, to explain why
they probably deserved some form of punishment. Casper writes that
defendants found it difficult to judge the fairness of their sentence in
abstract terms:

> Many were uncomfortable and confused in considering the ques-
> tion, 'do you think your sentence was fair?' Fairness is a concept

which is not – except in an often somewhat hollow and even wistful fashion – especially salient to the men with whom I spoke. Although a few had real concern about abstract concepts such as fairness or justice, most were concerned with the world as it is rather than as it might be. Thus, a 'fair' sentence was measured not against some abstract notion about what is just (for example, 'the punishment fits the crime' or 'equal punishment for crimes causing equal harm') but rather against reality. Thus, a 'fair' sentence meant largely two things to the men: (1) a good deal – something less than they might have gotten; (2) the going rate for an offence. (Casper, 1972, p. 89)

He found that defendants generally supported the existence of the laws they had offended against, and wished that they could be more law-abiding. However, this latter point, including the argument that defendants wished the criminal justice system were more effective in keeping them from crime is less well supported by the referenced data than his other findings.

Much of the subsequent research on offenders' perceptions of fairness is based on large-scale surveys instead of in-depth interviews. Casper himself conducted a research study in which 812 men were interviewed just after they were charged, 628 of whom were re-interviewed after their case had been completed (Casper, 1978). In this study he conceptualised fairness as having three dimensions: just desert – or the appropriateness of the treatment in each case, equality and the adequacy of the process by which decisions were made. He concluded that his interviewees used all three dimensions when deciding whether they thought their sentence was fair. A body of research that has emerged out of this work, but has been largely driven by Tyler is the one on procedural justice (Casper, Tyler and Fisher, 1988; Jackson, Tyler, Bradford, Taylor and Shiner, 2010; Sunshine and Tyler, 2003; Tyler, 1990, 1997, 2003, 2006, 2010). Procedural justice is defined as 'the fairness of the manner in which the authority was exercised' (Tyler, 2010, p. 127) and encompasses both the way in which decisions were arrived at and the way people felt they were treated in the course of this process (Tyler, 1990). The quality of decision making is perceived as high when authorities appear unbiased and give the case the attention it deserves (Tyler, 1990, 2003). Interpersonal treatment is perceived as positive when people feel treated with dignity and respect (Tyler, 2003, p. 298). The main conclusion of this literature is that procedural justice rather than the favourability of the outcome is the most important determinant in whether people see the way they are treated as fair (Jackson et al., 2010; Sunshine and Tyler, 2003). This literature has come to largely define the meaning of the term 'legitimacy' in the field of criminology, as:

> the widespread belief among members of the public (and inmates) that the police, the courts, the prisons and the legal system are authorities entitled to make decisions and who should be deferred to in matters of criminal justice. (Jackson et al., 2010, p. 4)

This definition of legitimacy explicitly excludes whether the decisions by authorities align with people's personal morality – the feeling that a law should be obeyed because it is just (Tyler, 1990) – although recently there have been attempts to re-integrate these concepts (Jackson et al., 2012).

Issues with the definition of legitimacy will be discussed in greater detail in Chapter 4, but here the question arises whether this supposed dominance of procedural justice is likely to be true in the case of long-term prisoners. If someone has received a sentence of ten years and thought the way he was treated in court was fair, but that his eventual sentence was overly harsh, will that make him see the sentence in a more favourable light than if it were the other way around? Or will it be neither the process nor the (formal) outcome but rather the lived experience of the sentence which determines his overall views? In the case of long prison sentences, where the outcome of a case lasts so much longer than the court process, it is questionable whether procedural justice in arriving at the sentence will weigh more heavily than distributive justice (and just deserts) in the offender's mind.

In addition, as Bottoms and Tankebe (2012) have pointed out, within prisons the outcomes of disciplinary decisions by the regime are likely to weigh more heavily in prisoners' evaluations of these decisions, because knowledge of outcomes is shared among large numbers of prisoners and outcomes can therefore be compared for fairness. The same is true for sentences themselves; prisoners are often in a position to assess distributive justice because they discuss and compare their sentences in relation to their offences. If Bottoms and Tankebe (2012) are right, this is likely to make the sentencing outcome more important. Other authors have pointed out that existing procedural justice and legitimacy research is limited because it has not considered all the factors which may play a role in building legitimacy, as well as neglecting the possibility that legitimacy is ascribed differently in individual cases than by the aggregates investigated (Smith, 2007). A recent volume that analyses the concept of legitimacy beyond procedural justice (Tankebe and Liebling, 2013) has included findings that distributive justice is *more* important than procedural justice in determining people's perceptions of the legality of the policy (Hough, Jackson and Bradford, 2013). Given that is likely that distributive justice in courts is of greater concern to the punished than the distributive justice in police outcomes to the general public, this further undermines the claim that procedural justice trumps other considerations. For these reasons, this book does not build on the procedural justice literature, beyond the recognition that procedural justice is likely to play a role in shaping people's views of their sentence.

While the importance of procedural justice has been studied extensively, the importance of perceptions of just deserts in sentence evaluations has received little attention. Only a handful of studies have attempted to separate just deserts (whether the sentence was substantively fair in its own right, given the offence) from offenders' expectations and comparisons of their sentences with those received by others. Krohn and Stratton (1980) asked 153 adult male prisoners questions about their views of their offence and found that, while 83 per cent admitted they were guilty and 70 per cent thought the law they had offended against was fair, only 22 per cent thought their actions had caused real harm and only 42 per cent that their punishment was fair. These results beg the question why people think laws are fair when they think offending against them does not cause harm, and whether it was the perception of not having caused harm or considerations of distributive justice that meant many thought their sentence was unfair. In a Canadian study, 53 young male offenders, who were either imprisoned or given probation, were surveyed to find out what they thought of their sentence (McWilliams and Pease, 1990). It was found that 62 per cent thought the sentence was what they deserved for their crime, while 70 per cent said their sentence matched their expectations. Between 14 and 19 per cent thought that their sentence was less than they deserved or expected. This suggests that the participants in this study *expected* slightly more punishment than they felt they *deserved*, but also that it may be the case that a sizeable minority of offenders feel that they deserve *more* punishment and not just because they had expected a harsher sentence. The authors of a further study found that while 19 of the 100 offenders surveyed thought their sentence was lenient and 41 thought their sentence was severe, 40 felt it was very fair (McGinnis and Carlson, 1981). In other research, 75 per cent of 387 people on periodic detention in New Zealand thought their sentence was fair (Searle, Knaggs and Simonsen, 2003), while half of 36 Norwegian prisoners felt it was right that they were in prison, but two thirds thought their sentence was too long (Kolstad, 1996).

In the above studies, the proportion of offenders who thought their sentence was fair varies widely (from 40 per cent to 75 per cent), along with the proportion considering their sentence lenient (from 2 per cent to 19 per cent). A further study focusing on the experiences of offenders found that 'the vast majority of both males and females felt that the sentences they received were too harsh' (Kratcoski and Scheijerman, 1974, p. 73), which does not align well with the other research findings. These discrepancies may be due to local differences, or changes over time, but may also be due to the problematic nature of using survey methods to explore topics of fairness and meaning (Liebling, 2004, p. 367), especially when these have not previously been investigated in an exploratory way. Asking a question such as 'do you think your sentence was fair', when so many little understood factors are likely to play a role, means that people may interpret the question in different ways, have different underlying reasons for their answers, and that slight alterations in formulation can lead to quite different results. When participants do not have the opportunity to elaborate their thinking, it is unclear, for example, whether they thought their sentence was unfair because they did not feel they had done any harm; because they had been promised a lighter sentence by their lawyer; because they felt the court procedures were flawed; or because they felt they should have been excused considering the circumstances. These surveys therefore fail to provide a full and rounded picture of *how* the punished evaluate their sentence, and what factors play a role in these evaluations. Because knowledge of how sentences are experienced by the punished is relatively underdeveloped, exploratory research is needed before questionnaires, with their restrictions on what can be asked and answered, are used to refine our understanding of questions that are already known to be meaningful in this context (see also Cohen and Taylor, 1972).

Some exploratory research is starting to emerge. One (partly) qualitative study was carried out in Australia (Indermaur, 1994). Fifty-three offenders were interviewed using a questionnaire that included some open-ended questions. When asked what 'fairness meant', respondents most often mentioned consistency (35 per cent), 27 per cent mentioned leniency or compassion, with 19 per cent feeling that for the sentence to be fair the judge had to take account of all the factors (and offenders' needs) in each case. Only 11 per cent felt that the punishment had to be proportionate to the crime committed. Fifty-eight per cent of respondents felt their sentence had been unfair, with the most common reason being that their personal circumstances had not been given sufficient consideration. Indermaur points to a tension between the emphasis placed on consistency and on the need to take individual circumstances into account, which arguably pull in opposite directions. This tension has also been observed in prison studies, with prisoners wanting prison regimes to be flexible, making decisions on the individual merits of each case, but to also be consistent (Crewe, 2009; Sparks et al., 1996). Other qualitative research on offenders' perceptions has taken place in the course of evaluations of particular sentencing initiatives. For example, an evaluation of the pilot of Community Reparation Orders in Scotland found that offenders who had been given this new sentence on the whole did not understand what the sentence meant or what it was meant to achieve. Also, more than half felt that the sentence had not been the right response to their crime (Curran et al., 2007). Even though in such research the discussion with offenders about the legitimacy or purpose of their punishment is often limited, it is still regrettable that these types of investigations are only carried out for new sentences.

Recently, a research project in Scotland has compared the views of community and short-term prison sentences by interviewing offenders who had experienced both, some in prison and some in the community (Armstrong and Weaver, 2010; Weaver and Armstrong, 2011). Because those in prison usually had a long history of short-term sentences, for them it was not so much their most recent sentence, but rather the *accumulation* of sentences that had a negative impact on their lives. Most reported only having been given one or two community penalties before a long list of periods of imprisonment. They felt that they were being judged on their criminal records, rather than on any positive changes they might have made in their lives. While some felt that prison had been positive and life-changing because it had allowed them to engage in programmes or because it had given them motivation to overcome their drug habit, most endured their time in prison passively, enduring routine and boredom. For many, imprisonment had become a normal feature of their lives, and there was evidence of a progression towards anger and hopelessness with a greater accumulation of sentences.

Other research has focused on prisoner attitudes towards the criminal justice system, rather than towards their sentence. The consensus seems to be that such attitudes tend to deteriorate during incarceration due to the adverse conditions experienced, at least in the US (Franke et al., 2010). In a recent narrative research project violent offenders positioned the criminal justice system as one of the main adversaries in their tales of heroic struggle, in which they struggled 'alone, against particular, and particularly formidable forces, to achieve their goals' (Presser, 2009, p. 106) and in which 'the wrongdoing the men had done was dwarfed by the greater wrongs done to them by the justice system' (Presser, 2009, p. 120). These findings suggest that many prisoners feel that they are treated unfairly, but it is not clear whether this is due to their treatment in the prison or their negative perception of their sentence.

The experience of (long-term) imprisonment

In contrast to the scarcity of research on perceptions of the sentence imposed, there is an extensive literature on 'how the prison experience is lived and what shapes it' (Liebling, 2004, p. 145). With the focus of this book on long-term imprisonment, some of this literature is pertinent to the questions it aims to address. Earlier studies (e.g., McCorkle and Korn, 1954; Sykes, 1958; Wheeler, 1961) focused on subcultures in the prison and the way men organised themselves when forced to live together. They examined the way in which prisoner relationships with other prisoners and with staff were constituted, how an inmate code developed and whether this was a result of the institution or the values prisoners brought into the prison with them (importation). Prison studies have also been interested in the problem of order; why there is not more disorder in prisons given that people are held against their will, and what factors lead to order breaking down (Carrabine, 2004; Mathiesen, 1965; Sparks et al., 1996; Sykes, 1958). Some of these studies have focused on the legitimacy of the regime, linking this to staff–prisoner relationships, the provision of material goods and visits and the way in which power in prison is operationalised (Carrabine, 2004; Sparks et al., 1996).

Alison Liebling and her research group at the Prisons Research Centre at Cambridge have taken this work forward by arguing that there is more to the quality of prison life than legitimacy and have developed new methods to study what they call the 'moral performance' of prison regimes (Liebling, 2004, 2011). Through the use of Appreciative Inquiry (AI), they have explored with prison staff and prisoners what the prison experience should ideally be like, comparing this with what it was actually like at the time of the research. This work is an example of how mixed methods research can make a major contribution to our understanding of prisoners' experiences. Based on the qualitative work a questionnaire was developed and then piloted. The eventual questionnaire (the Measure of the Quality of Prison Life – MQPL) made it possible to ask large numbers of respondents about aspects of their experience that were demonstrably meaningful to them. This research identified four aspects of the prison experience that determine the quality of prison life: dimensions of staff–prisoner relationships, regime dimensions (the level of family contact, opportunities for personal development and feelings of personal safety, amongst others), social structure dimensions (power and social life) and individual items of meaning and quality of life. Interestingly, a single item on the questionnaire investigating whether prisoners found their imprisonment meaningful was often answered with 'neither agree nor disagree', leading Liebling to conclude that questions of meaning might be difficult to answer using structured responses (2004, p. 367).

A recent ethnographic study by Crewe (2009) has drawn the different strands of prison research together by examining adaptation to imprisonment, the social world within prison and how power within the prison is used and perceived. As the title of his book *'The Prisoner Society'* suggests, his findings aim to provide an overall picture of prison life as it is in the 21st century in one prison in England. The main argument of the book is that the way penal power operates has changed from authoritarian but consistent decision making (with little input from the prisoner) to more discretionary decisions which are based on all aspects of the prisoner's conduct. This change, Crewe argues, has significant consequences for the experience of prisoners.

This body of work, while not directly related to prisoners' perceptions of their sentence, does provide valuable insight into the experience of imprisonment. It especially supports the finding by Patrick and Marsh (2001) and Halsey (2007) discussed above, that the way in which prisoners are treated during their sentence has an impact on how they make sense of it and highlights that this can vary from prison to prison. Sparks et al. (1996) examined experiences of the regime in two different long-term prisons, comparing a relatively 'relaxed' prison, Long Lartin, with one where the regime was seen as much more austere, Albany. Their respondents are quoted as seeing Albany as a 'punishment' prison, rather than as the 'rehabilitation' prison they think the management would like it to be (pp. 189–190). Similarly, Liebling (2004) compared the different cultures in five prisons and found substantial differences in staff–prisoner relationships and regime dimensions. Those held in prisons where there was little interaction or trust between staff and prisoners, where they were shown little respect and felt that procedures were unfair, were more likely to agree with the statement 'my time here seems very much like a punishment' (p. 348). She also reported that some prisoners found meaning in their sentence because they felt they had been listened to, had progressed on educational goals, or had avoided a worse fate of death or continued drug addiction. Nonetheless, over a third agreed with the statement 'my experience of prison is meaningless' (p. 367), although, as noted above many neither agreed nor disagreed.

A qualitative study of staff–prisoner relationships in Whitemoor (a high security prison) (Liebling, Arnold and Straub, 2011), supports Comfort's (2008) and Ashkar and Kenny's (2008) findings that many prisoners have a wish for rehabilitation, which is not supported through rehabilitative input from the regime. The long-term prisoners interviewed at Whitemoor wanted to 'reinvent' themselves during their long-term sentence, in order to make a positive future more likely (p. 34). However, the resources necessary to capitalise on this willingness to change and, crucially, positive recognition of their motivation from the regime were largely lacking. Both staff and prisoners wished that Whitemoor were a more rehabilitative institution and felt that in order for it to become so, more attention would have to be paid to the individual prisoner and their situation, rather than the current sole focus on cognitive behavioural programmes.

The research on imprisonment furthermore suggests that features of the prison environment might make a serious and critical examination of one's sentence difficult. Carrabine (2004) and Sparks et al. (1996) have pointed out that the reality and imposed routines of imprisonment can make power relations in the prison seem inevitable, which means that these often go unquestioned. Prisoners accept them as such, rather than as legitimate. Crewe's findings (2009) suggest that the legitimacy of the actual sentence may also remain unexamined by many prisoners. In his typology of coping with imprisonment, 'enthusiasts' accept their sentence as fair and denounce their former self, while 'pragmatists' do not reflect on the morality of their crime or the legitimacy of their punishment, but take their situation for granted. 'Stoics' are critical of the way power is exercised in the prison, but keep quiet in order to make life easier for themselves. 'Retreatists', often drug addicts, are resigned to a life of repeated imprisonment and therefore do not question their sentence. Only 'Players' (about one in four of the prisoners Crewe came across) really resist the regime, but they do so covertly; they try to manipulate systems to their own advantage. Crewe argues that, with the incentive schemes currently in place in prisons and collective time reduced through the provision of televisions and PlayStations in the cells, there is now little prisoner solidarity and therefore little collective resistance (2009, p. 231). His typology means that only Stoics and Players might oppose their sentence on moral grounds, since Enthusiasts accept it for moral reasons and Pragmatists and Retreatists do not reflect on the fairness of their sentence at all. Earlier research also suggested that opposition to one's sentence may be rare: Sykes wrote that 'the criminal in prison seldom denies the legitimacy of confinement' (1958, p. 47) and that prisoners see their sentence as a consequence of their own mistakes, the police outwitting them or just pure chance.

Conclusion

This chapter has outlined what is known about the way people who have been sentenced evaluate and give meaning to their sentences. As noted above, the literature is fragmented; often papers reporting similar findings do not reference each other. While there is some excellent qualitative exploratory work available (e.g., Comfort, 2008; Halsey, 2007), this has tended to address questions of fairness and meaning only in passing. However, although a comprehensive picture of how people understand their sentence has yet to be developed, there are recurring themes. Feeling treated unfairly and disrespectfully during the court process (Casper, 1972; Rijksen, 1958; Sunshine and Tyler, 2003; Tyler, 1990, 2003), not feeling like the case is being treated on its individual merits (Armstrong and Weaver, 2010; Indermaur, 1994; Weaver and Armstrong, 2011), and perceptions of inconsistency (Casper, 1972; Indermaur, 1994), are all associated with feelings of injustice. During the prison sentence a lack of structured activity and adverse conditions are likely to lead to feelings of hostility towards the justice system (Franke et al., 2010; Presser, 2008). The link between offenders' own views of the morality of their conduct and perceptions of fairness is less clear.

In exploring penal purposes, the literature so far suggests that rehabilitation is the aim of punishment most supported by offenders (Ashkar and Kenny, 2008; Comfort, 2008; Liebling et al., 2011), followed by deterrence (Halsey, 2007; Rex, 2005). Within prison, perceptions of rehabilitation are linked to positive staff–prisoner relationships (Liebling, 2004; Patrick and Marsh, 2001; Sparks et al., 1996), but often offenders feel rehabilitation is not achieved due to a lack of support and individual attention (Halsey, 2007; Liebling et al., 2011). In the community, staff–offender relationships are also important; those that are genuine, care-oriented and non-judgemental are experienced as most rehabilitative (Appleton, 2010; Barry, 2006, 2007). Deterrence is seen by some as an important factor in their decision to move away from crime, but deterrence is not often effective partly because, in the context of bleak lives outside, the prison environment is not sufficiently aversive (Halsey, 2007). Prisons research has shown that prison conditions (including its dull routines) (Carrabine, 2004; Sparks et al., 1996), adaptation strategies and the lack of time prisoners spend together (Crewe, 2009) can limit (collective) opposition to sentences. Moreover, the literature suggests that it is not only features of the court process and imprisonment that shape prisoners' views of their sentence, but also their own aims and hopes for the future (Ashkar and Kenny, 2008; Comfort, 2008).

Against the background of existing knowledge and theory described in this chapter, this book aims to bring together the different research strands discussed and to fill in some of the significant gaps in the literature. For example, why might someone feel that their sentence is fair when they do not think they harmed anyone? And how are prisoners' interpretations of their punishment shaped by their wider lives? In order to find answers to such questions, it was important to solicit prisoners' own views, rather than asking them to select from a set range of responses, and to gain an understanding grounded in their own narrative about their lives.

3
Purposes Perceived in the Sentence

Introduction

This chapter examines to what extent justifications of punishment find expression in prisoners' accounts of their sentence. Consequently, the starting point for analysis is 'etic' (Silverman, 2001) – it largely draws on concepts originating from sources external to the research. In the next two chapters, these views will be put into context, drawing on the participants' overall narrative of their sentence, within which perceptions of purpose did not always sit easily. For example, criticisms about prison failing in its aim to rehabilitate did not translate into critical accounts of imprisonment. Such tensions between purposes perceived and overall narratives will also be examined in the subsequent chapters.

The concepts around which the material here is organised originate from the philosophical literature and policy documents on the purposes of punishment in general and imprisonment in particular; they include rehabilitation, deterrence and incapacitation (consequentialist justifications of punishment) and retribution. Perhaps because (a mix of) these are most often cited as the purpose of punishment in the public domain and have currency in our cultural discourse (Miller and Glassner, 1997), these aims could all be detected in the interviewees' statements about the purpose of their imprisonment. In order to reflect which purposes were most (spontaneously) represented in the men's accounts, the discussion in this chapter starts with the most salient purposes of rehabilitation and reform and moves towards less well-developed themes, ending with incapacitation.

To explore the links between justifications of punishment and the lived experience of those who are punished, it is necessary to recognise instances of the former in the talk of men who only rarely used terms such as 'rehabilitation' or 'incapacitation'. In doing so, I draw upon the work of Rex (2005). She expressed each justification of punishment in a simple statement for her survey of different groups of criminal justice actors about their views and preferences. Her definitions are used as a starting point in each section, as they tend to capture the way in which the purposes were expressed in the interviews quite well. When the way the men spoke about their sentence differed significantly from her definitions, this is discussed.

Rehabilitation and reform

Rehabilitation has many different, sometimes contradictory, meanings (McNeill, 2013). These include effecting change (or reintegration) for the offender's own good, motivated by concern for his or her welfare; managerialist approaches focusing on risk management and harm reduction, motivated by consequentialist considerations (Robinson, 2008); and restoring offenders to full citizenship (McNeill, 2012). Besides differences in motivation and ultimate purpose, many writers (Carlen and Worrall, 2004; Duff, 2001; Rex, 2005) make a distinction between reform, which focuses on the offenders' moral dispositions, and rehabilitation, which changes the likelihood of further offending in other ways. For example, Duff defines reform as changing 'people's dispositions and motives'(2001, p. 5), while he describes rehabilitation as 'improv[ing] people's skills, capacities and opportunities' (2001, p. 5). In Rex's research, reform and rehabilitation were expressed as 'get them to change their ways' and 'help them with problems behind their offending' (2005, p. 86) respectively. Other relevant texts (Comfort, 2008; Crewe, 2009; Scottish Prison Service, 2011) do not make this distinction, instead referring to both aims as rehabilitation. In the interviews, the men also tended to use the term 'rehabilitation' to capture both concepts (no one mentioned reform) or more descriptive phrases, such as 'change me as a person' (David) or 'anything to benefit myself' (Gordon). However, a distinction was apparent: the men described attempts to make reoffending less likely that focused on internal problems, such as problem solving skills or anger management, but also felt they needed help with more practical problems, like accommodation and employment, in order to be able to move away from offending. To capture this, the term 'rehabilitation' is used below to describe help with practical problems external to the offender, but including substance misuse.

Rehabilitation, in any of its guises, played a part in almost all the interviewees' accounts and was brought up spontaneously as one of the (desired) purposes of imprisonment by men in each of the three groups (those at the start of their sentence, those at the end and those on licence). Of all the possible purposes of criminal punishment, it played by far the largest part in the stories told and held the most meaning for the interviewees. However, many were disappointed in the prison's efforts to achieve rehabilitation. In fact, this was the topic that raised the most anger and criticism of the regime in the interviews. In what follows, I focus first on the reform of character, temper, reactions and thoughts. After this I examine the extent to which the interviewees felt they were rehabilitated, supported practically to successfully move away from their previous lives.

Reform

Most of the men supported the aim of reform; they wanted help with their offending behaviour, their explosive tempers, unhelpful thoughts or a combination of these. Dan was somewhat unusual in that he presented himself as *still* in need of reform:

> DAN: It would be nice if we could come up with a technical answer or even a medical one, they can give you injections, it would stop Dan to be the Dan before he got the injection. If I was returned to being a normal member of society.
> MS: Then you would take that injection?
> DAN: Well, I would jump at it, I would volunteer to try the first one. I don't want to be in prison, I don't want to assault people, but I've done it, I can't change it, I can't turn the clock back.

In contrast, most of the interviewees told a story of having already been reformed in one way or another (see further below), presenting themselves as 'good' at the time of the interview (Presser, 2008) or at least as better than they were.

> Aye, I think I've changed, you know what I mean, I really do think I have changed. I think this sentence has opened my eyes up to a lot of things. Just, the way I look at life, stop being selfish, stop thinking about myself all the time. (Graham)

There also were several interviewees who felt that reform was not a proper purpose for imprisonment in their case, because they had never been 'bad people' or criminals. This included all the interviewees who were imprisoned for their first offence, namely Devan, Robert,[1] David and Paul. Alan, who had had a conventional career and life outside of prison, had been convicted once before but also felt that he was essentially non-criminal and did not need to be reformed. Yet denying the reformative purpose of imprisonment often made it difficult for them to make sense of their sentence.

> I've asked myself [what my sentence is meant to achieve], well not [sighs]. I've sat down and spoken about it with my boss and he's asked me/ in his own words 'it was a pointless sentence', because it's not going to change anything, it was an accident. (David)

David's quoting a third party suggests that he found it difficult to personally declare his sentence pointless, but his lack of disagreement suggests that he does indeed see his sentence as lacking purpose. This illustrates how essential an element of reform (or rehabilitation) is to the meaning prisoners ascribe to their sentence.

Cognitive behavioural courses

The men described reform within the prison as almost exclusively delivered through cognitive behavioural courses. Several of the interviewees credited such courses with changing their outlook on life. They tended to refer to a particular interaction they had had with course facilitators, which had forced them to re-examine the way they reacted in certain situations.

> So we end up/ they challenged me on it again and we're fighting through it and fighting through it. I was adamant it was the right thing to do, was to attack the person. So I says 'she's sitting there with a guy having a drink, why did she not tell you that on the phone? When she phones you 'I'm sitting here with such and such'. And they said 'what about if that person that she is sitting there drinking with, it turned out it was her cousin?' I was stuck in that position like that [freezes] I'm caught out there, you know what I mean, there was nothing I could say or do, because I've already done the guy, but that was the sort of scenario they put you in, you know? (Gordon)

The detail in this description shows how important the interaction described was in initiating change for Gordon. The ease and enthusiasm with which he related this story, not being a great storyteller in the rest of the interview, suggests that he had told it before (Hydén, 2008), reflected upon it and saw it as a pivotal moment. A few others also recounted moments in which their world-view had been challenged by cognitive behavioural courses.

On the other hand, the majority of the men felt that the reliance on cognitive behavioural courses to deliver reform was problematic. The assessment procedures for courses were seen by some as less than robust, with psychometric tests easily subverted.

> I know for a fact everybody was just writing/ just putting the answer in they obviously knew they wanted to hear. It's like you're manipu-lating the system, the prisoners, you know what I mean, so for me that's not a good sign. (Andy)

Furthermore, several interviewees questioned the courses' efficacy because, like Halsey's participants (2007), they felt the courses did not go into enough depth and were unrealistic about situations outside the prison.

> Useful information, but to be honest I think in the heat of the moment, I don't really/ when I think back to all the times I've lost my temper, the things that you're taught in anger management don't pop into my head, so I don't really see it as helpful, to be honest. (Mohammed)

A commonly expressed view was that, rather than being truly aimed at reform, the purpose of cognitive behavioural courses was to keep the government or the electorate happy.

> But my opinion and for what I've seen through the years, gener-ally I think the courses that they've got in prison for them to say to people that they were trying to rehabilitate people. It's just number crunching really, it's just eehm making them look good. (Lino)
>
> See all like these daft courses and all that, that's just so the newspaper can't write stuff about the jail, so it covers the jail like 'aye, we're helping them with courses and that'. (Doug)

Here the men's accounts seemed to match sociological theories of criminal justice in which the state is described as posturing to emphasise its own efficacy and power (Garland, 1996) rather than enacting normative theo-ries. This was interesting, as overall the men were not critical of the use of imprisonment and drew very little on sociological understandings of crime and justice. In this respect they resembled informants in other prison research projects (e.g., Crewe, 2009; Mathiesen, 1965; Sykes, 1958).

One reason for the critical tone about the reformative efforts made by the prison was the tension between the importance of attending courses and the unresponsiveness of these courses to individual timelines and needs. Attending required courses played a large role in the progression to a lower risk classification, open prison and parole (see Crewe, 2009 for an in-depth analysis of how a shift towards neo-paternalist power in prisons has transformed the way prisoners have to engage with their sentence). Courses therefore also became an *obstacle* to progression when it was not possible to access them in time for significant moments in the sentence, such as becoming eligible for a move to the open estate. Chris's account provides a good example of how courses could delay rather than facilitate progress:

> Basically as soon as I've finished the course then I can move on to trying to get the open [prison] and trying to get this college thing done, but my timing is a bit off, so, because you need to put in for it before September, so if I don't get it in, then whatever, ... I've only got to do certain courses so it's only ten weeks I've got to do, but it's just (.) actually just trying to get onto it, you know what I mean. (Chris)

Chris said that his timing was 'a bit off', ostensibly resigned to the way the prison works. However, for him as well as for others, it was not only the timing but also the lack of fit between the way he saw his situation and the resources on offer that rankled. Later in the interview Chris expressed frustration that he was being held back from accessing the support he thought he needed.

> Cause it's a bit weird really, something I want to do that will help me with my drug problem, but they're holding me back from doing it, to do a drug course, you know what I mean? So but/ well you can't do anything and there's nobody you can speak to or anything to actually speed things up, apparently it just works on your parole date, so however far your parole date away is, it works on that really.

Chris's frustration was palpable: the system did not respond to his individual needs and he was powerless to change it. Several others, conversely, had been assessed as needing a course they felt they did not need. For example Alan, who had been convicted of a drug offence but did not have a drug problem himself, was unsure why he needed to take the Substance Related Offending Behaviour (SROB) course. Lino questioned why he had to attend a course on violence when he had not violently offended for years and had already completed the same course in the past. These mismatches between the men's perceptions of their own needs and what they were offered (or required to do) fed into the view that courses were not truly aimed at helping individual prisoners.

Making courses essential for progression inevitably meant that many prisoners attended them solely for this reason, rather than out of a desire to actually engage with the material on offer. This in turn was perceived as having a negative impact on what could be achieved in the classroom.

> No, it's sort of that, up there, it's just a numbers game. And they sort of try to frighten you with: you don't do that, you don't get your parole. People do it and people just go on and sit in a class and just say nothing. And they can't do nothing because the boy's just sitting there, y'know. (Graham)

Graham's quote illustrates how, by making courses compulsory for progression, formal compliance (meeting the minimum requirements, 'just sitting there') rather than substantive compliance (actively engaging with what is on offer (Robinson and McNeill, 2008)) was encouraged. In addition, courses being compulsory meant that they were often oversubscribed so that those who wanted the intervention on offer (and would have substantively complied) but were not assessed as requiring it were not able to get a place. Finally, because prisoners attended courses in order to progress, they evaluated them on this basis:

> They may work for some people, but then again, we were all different people. In my case, they done nothing for me, I mean I got nothing out of the system for (biding) all they courses, I got no parole, I got no open estate. (Dan)

The question arises whether, when a course has been successful in making the prisoner reflect on their behaviour or thoughts (as it was for Gordon) but then fails to deliver in terms of progression, the prisoner continues to make the effort necessary to achieve permanent behavioural change, and thereby perceives himself as reformed, or retrospectively dismisses the course as useless and returns to his previous behaviours.

Conflicting views about whether cognitive behavioural courses achieved reform did not only occur across the interviews, but also *within* them. This warrants attention, for inconsistencies can provide clues about the influences on what the men were able to say on this topic.

One of those with contradictory views, Graham, who was quoted as saying courses are 'just a numbers game' above, also said:

> Aye, that was a SROBS course, it's substance related offending behaviour and it (.) it made me look at (.) I didn't think about the boy's family I had killed, you know, and it made me look at that, y'know, and it asked how do I feel and what bits are my triggers and all that ... I don't know, this sentence has made me look at things a lot, a lot clearer (.). Maybe had a good look at my life and do I want to keep on using drugs. I don't, that's why I done the course, the drug course, to give me a better understanding what my triggers are.

When I pointed out the inconsistency, he tried to make his views compatible by saying:

> No, aye, 'cause I, [the course] was good/ everybody all get getting on and interacting with everybody, y'know, that was good y'know, but you have to get in with certain boys, that you can get on with, y'know.

In Graham's case, his view of the courses as helpful seemed to play a bigger part in his overall account than the more critical view of courses as a cynical exercise on the part of prison administrators. He mentioned having benefited from attending a course right at the start of the interview and generally told a story that was in keeping with this; of having changed because of his imprisonment. The more critical view surfaced in the interview as follows:

> So, [a long term sentence] is totally different (.) and it's better, y'know? And now, now that I've done, there's courses to do, but it's obviously about what it's/ it's a number game for them, for the courses. That's all, they just want to fill the seats, and they're (.) they've been 'oh you do that and you'll get your parole'.

In this one short quote, two distinct voices are evident: an enthusiastic and hopeful voice speaking until 'there's courses to do', after which a more critical voice takes over, sounding like a cynical old prison-hand who knows the ropes and sees through the intentions of his jailors. Here Graham seems to draw on an institutional or group discourse amongst prisoners (Miller and Glassner, 1997). Prisoners are likely to discuss courses amongst themselves, and the similarity in the men's depictions of the true purpose of courses being the placation of the government or the public suggests that negative views may predominate in these discussions. The discrepancy between the dominant group view and his own experience may have led to Graham's conflicted account.

On the other hand, the courses themselves influenced what the interviewees had to say about them at times, as was clear from the use of words such as 'triggers', 'impulsive behaviour' and 'problem solving'. It was those who were most positive about the reform achieved who most adopted the courses' language. However, adopting the course discourse (so to speak) could also lead to contradictory accounts. Some of the men were enthusiastic about courses, but provided impoverished accounts of how they had benefited.

> JAMES: I never thought about the long-term. It was the problem-solving course that I done that helped [me over] that.
>
> MS: So did the course make you think about that? How did it do that, how did it help you?
>
> JAMES: It made me think about (.) foreseeing problems in the future. And what can be causing those problems. I thought you're supposed to write all this down? [laughs]

> MALCOLM: But as I say, I done cog skills before, I benefited that, like I thought it was alright ken, I thought it was alright.
>
> MS: How do you think you benefited?
>
> MALCOLM: Mmm (.) I just (.) I learned about a lot more, ken, about all your problem solving and just eeeh/ och I don't know basically just (.) phew, honestly I don't know. I can't/ I just DID, I just did benefit out of it, it just made me kind of a better person, ken.

The way in which James closed down the discussion of the benefits of the courses he had taken makes it clear that this was not a topic about which he had a lot to say or on which he had reflected. Similarly, Malcolm was not able to articulate an answer to my question. This mirrors McKendy's (2006) findings that men in prison often tell fragmented and inconsistent accounts because they have to marry their own experiences of deprivation with the discourses promoted by the prison, notably taking responsibility for their crimes. The desirability of having successfully completed cognitive behavioural courses will be very clear for prisoners hoping to progress in their sentence. They therefore might try to incorporate this into their account, even though they are not sure *how* exactly it has benefited them. A further factor may also play a role in the interviewees' positive descriptions of courses, namely their desire to tell a positive story about their imprisonment (see Chapter 5).

Individual approaches vs. managerialism

The only other reformative effort made by the regime mentioned by the men was individual support from staff members. This type of support was desired more than it was delivered, but there were some instances, albeit mostly in the past, when interviewees felt this had benefited them.

> I think I got a lot of help when I was in [another prison] with seeing a psychiatrist and that, all through your sentence. I think that helped, talking to, meeting somebody once a week talking to them and getting a bit of talk, communicating, going. But in here you get nothing. (Ian)

My interviews with those with long histories of imprisonment may have captured the posited shift from penal welfarism to managerialism (Cheliotis, 2006; Crewe, 2009; Feeley and Simon, 1992; Robinson, 2008), with the logic underpinning prisons moving from one that saw crimes as stemming from social problems, therefore necessitating an understanding of individual prisoners' lives, to an economic logic with a focus on being cost effective, measured through performance targets (Crewe, 2009). Whether this change is really as all-encompassing and clear-cut as suggested is a subject of much debate (Crewe, 2009; Kruttschnitt and Gartner, 2005), and, as discussed in the introduction, there is no one clear rationale underpinning imprisonment in Scotland. However, the transition to managerialism did find expression in my interviewee's accounts. None of the men had benefited from the kind of sustained professional attention described by Ian during their most recent sentence. Mark's experience with a social worker came the closest.

> I had a relationship with a social worker in [another prison] for about 16 month and he had a good impact on me because he actually pointed out the 'poor me' the 'selfish me' you know, actually starting to think about other folk with my actions.

While this relationship was relatively enduring, it is not clear how intense the support was. Others who credited interactions with prison staff tended to refer to either prison officers or education staff and did not go into detail about how these had changed them, but emphasised the importance of feeling that someone was interested in them as a person.

> Yeah, just they take an interest in where you are going and that and what you've got to do, whereas in [another prison] they never, they didn't. (Colin)

However, the majority of descriptions of interactions within the prison with social workers were negative – and highlighted that the men felt that even in one-to-one encounters they were not seen as individuals.

> But again, you've listened to me but I don't get asked these questions anywhere else in the jail so nobody really (.) I mean your social worker fair enough, but she just takes what information she has, she won't sit like this and listen, so you don't/ you get (.) categorized, you know what I mean, not how bad a drug dealer are you, you're just a drug dealer. (Alan)

The tension between the interviewees' wish for individual attention and its scarcity echoes others' findings that many prisoners want help and are frustrated by the prison's focus on risk assessment and cognitive behavioural courses (Crewe, 2009; Liebling et al., 2011). The discrepancy is especially troublesome considering that the men I spoke to generally presented themselves as being highly motivated to change. When people want to turn their lives around but are disappointed by the help on offer, an opportunity might be missed. Crewe characterises his prisoners' wanting help as evidence that they had been 'subsumed by official discourse' (2009, p. 120). I have also discussed above how the language of cognitive behavioural courses might have influenced what my informants had to say. However, for several of the men their problems in coping with the world, and especially avoiding conflict, were important themes in their accounts and added difficulty to their lives beyond the more structural constraints they experienced. These problems may have very well been a consequence of disadvantage and social exclusion, although they themselves tended not to make this link, but would need addressing over and above issues such as poverty and homelessness. In addition, the fact that the men did not accept that courses were the best way to address their problems shows that they had not completely accepted the prison's conception of their deficits and the best way to overcome them. Several of the men described how they thought reform *should* work, which always involved intensive individual input.

> They should try and rehabilitate you. If they can't rehabilitate you, talk to you and see what's going on in your head and try and get the right people in the right positions to help you and try and help you not to come back. (Stephen)

The more managerialist approach taken in prison was explicitly noted and regretted by many.

> Well, that's it, yeah, everyone's kinda classed as a group rather than as an individual. They don't have the resources to kinda really study on one person. (Paul)

In fact, it was in describing their view of the prison's input in reform (and rehabilitation) that the men were at their most critical, even though few went on to create a sustained critical account throughout the interview (see Chapter 4). Usually the language in which they expressed their views on this topic reflected their feeling that their lives were being dealt with much too lightly.

> ANDY: [Imprisonment] it's/ we'll no deal with it we'll just lock you away then we'll pop you back out in a few years, you know what I mean, hopefully you've changed that's the way I see it.
> MS: So you just have to do it on your own, type thing?
> ANDY: Change if you can, if you can't, we'll see you again once you come back.

Andy's 'we'll *just* lock you away' and 'we'll *pop* you back out' were mirrored by similar expressions by others, such as Chris saying that in prison 'people can be *brushed* away and...took out of people's minds'. Being treated as mere parts of an aggregate was painful to the men, who not only felt treated without the respect due to individuals, but also that the managerialist approach meant prison failed in its aims of rehabilitation and reform, with consequences for their lives beyond prison:

> I've been in the jail four year eight month, I'm getting out of the jail with £52 nothing, one set of clothes, that's it, you are flinging me out the door with nothing...and it's always the same when you say (.) they always turn around and say to you 'Oh aye, you slipped through the net this time' you know what I'm talking about, *you're just like a wheel in a cog*, that's what more or less it is [sounds the most aggressive here, also visibly upset]. (Ian, emphasis added)

In this they agreed with the participants in other research projects, who also overwhelmingly felt that their imprisonment did not achieve rehabilitation (Crewe, 2009; Halsey, 2007; Liebling et al., 2011; Liebling, 2004). In total, eight interviewees characterised their incarceration as a managerialist project, similar to the Scottish Prison Commission's (2008) view of imprisonment as warehousing. The Commission report only portrayed short-term sentences as warehousing, with long-term sentences characterised as having much greater opportunity to change prisoners. The men's experiences suggest, however, that despite the availability of courses, the prison experience of at least some long-term prisoners is also one of little meaningful input into rehabilitation and reform and of missed opportunities to support change.

Unlike the critical comments about cognitive behavioural courses, the critical views around managerialism drew on the men's own experiences. They expressed different views that centred on the same theme, and used different words to express these views, rather than repeating more or less the same point. These critical views are therefore much less likely to have been the result of a group discourse. There were again occasions, though, where the critical view sat in uneasy tension with more supportive views of reform or rehabilitation within the prison (for example, compare Andy's quote above with the ones in the following section).

'As if' reform

Several of the interviewees perceived reform in elements of their imprisonment where there was none intended. The main such element that was imbued with reformative powers was having time for reflection. While this used to be a major and intentional feature of penitentiaries, where the incarcerated were kept in almost total isolation (Garland, 1990), now time spent alone in the cell is more often characterised as detracting from the aims of imprisonment. For example, a recent Inspection Report noted:

> Opportunities for work and education are insufficient, causing long periods when … prisoners are 'locked up'. This situation is particularly *bad* for prisoners … on remand and at weekends. (HM Inspectorate of Prisons, 2010, p. 1, emphasis added)

While this negative view presumably only applies to excessively long periods of time in one's cell, given that time 'locked up' is a basic feature of most forms of imprisonment, time spent in solitary reflection is not mentioned in relevant SPS documents as a mechanism through which change may be effected (Scottish Prison Service, 2011). Nevertheless, having time to think was mentioned in passing as a purpose or effect of imprisonment by nine interviewees and played a major role in the understanding of their reform for James and Dan, both of whom were coming towards the end of their sentence.

But (.) that's one thing about prison, you have plenty of time on your hands to think. You do an awful lot of thinking in prison. If you can maybe apply that principle outside, you wouldn't even be in prison, but we don't spend the same time to think outside. Life is too full of other things, here you've got plenty of time on your hands. (Dan)

This view of reform closely echoes the findings of Comfort (2008) in her work on Californian prisoners. Some of her interviewees also latched on to having had time for reflection to make an account of successful reform possible, even in the absence of actual reformative intervention. Comfort writes that her interviewees 'retroactively make sense of periods of incarceration, and in so doing salvage aspects of that experience that can be recast in a positive light' (2008, p. 259), and thereby draw on 'as if' discourses of reform. Ashkar and Kenny (2008) also found that prisoners, in their case young offenders, looked for meaning in their sentence and often saw it as affording time for reflection and leading to positive change. Dan and James did the same, although only James actually constructed an account of personal change; Dan's account was much more ambivalent and fatalistic, as illustrated by his quote on page 31 above.

Time for reflection was not the only aspect of imprisonment imbued with reformative power. Andy's account provides a good illustration of how elements of imprisonment can be made to fit individual needs (or even vice versa), so that on the whole the prison experience can be seen as positive. Andy spent a substantial part of his interview trying to explain how the discipline in prison and access to the gym had made him a better person. In essence, he felt the discipline and having to follow rules had put him in his place, while the gym had given him much-needed self-confidence. Compare the following:

I think it's discipline, I think that's what a lot of people's missing, I think that's what I was missing eeehm, and the jail gave me that, because I'd no choice but to just do what I was told and it taught me sort of to comply with the rules and do whatever people wanted, do you know what I mean.... My dad had left the house, I was like 15 and I just took control of the house, like I mean, I was a big guy so I ran the show, I did whatever I wanted and when I got the jail it just really brought me down a peg.

And the gym really did help, I mean I says to [my social worker] and that as well when I first got out 'I really feel the gym is a positive thing for guys, especially boys who feel the need to carry a knife, because it can all to be with a lack of self-confidence'.

The contradiction in needing both to be put in his place and greater self-confidence was grounded in the way Andy presented his past self in the interview: as 'a big guy who ran the show', but also as follows:

> I always saw myself as a wee small boy in a sorta (.) against big guys out there. Even though I might have been bigger or whatever. And I always felt I needed the weapon, cause it gave me just the/ it evened up the odds for me, do you know what I mean, I felt it took away my size and that, so I had the knife, it gave me the same power as a big guy. I could even fight huge guys with a knife, put it that way, you're no scared, I mean that's the way it is.

These selves may be compatible, if the one represents his public and outward self; the big and fearless guy – a force to be reckoned with; while the other is his internal experience of himself – a frightened wee boy who has to work hard to maintain his outward persona. It is striking that Andy found aspects of imprisonment to fit both of these selves and to rehabilitate them, so that he was able to see himself as irrevocably changed by his time in prison.

In a further instance of 'as if' reform, Peter saw the support and good advice from older prisoners as the source of his reform. Rather than prison being a 'school of crime' (Halsey, 2007; Clemmer, 1970 cited in LeBel, Burnett, Maruna and Bushway, 2008, p. 134), he had been given pro-social messages by older prisoners. This was obviously not part of the reformative efforts made by the regime, however, and he did not perceive it as such. In his account, mentions of staff were absent in relation to reform, but other prisoners had taught him to avoid confrontation.

> I've learned stuff from other people, you know what I mean, and I'm not going on about a criminal way. I've learned to fucking control my anger, eeeh, not to (.) fucking like, get into confrontations with people, like, just try and walk away and get away from it, whereas before I would've just went/ just the sort of things I've learned, I, I try and avoid them now. (Peter)

There were elements of this in others' accounts too, in which prisoners were often portrayed as a pro-social rather than as a criminogenic influence (see also Lifers Public Safety Committee, 2004), but only in Peter's account did they play a pivotal part in the reform process.

Reform achieved?

Whether interviewees felt they had been reformed by their sentence was a more complicated question than it first appeared. First of all, it was a different question for those on licence and those still in prison. While still incarcerated, it can be difficult to assess to what extent one has changed. Chris noted this himself in relation to his drug use:

> I get a good feeling about saying no [to drugs] and that, yeah. So eehm (.), so it's a good feeling really, but at the same time I don't know whether I've overcome things completely YET, until maybe I get to the open prison.

On the other hand, it was by abstinence from drugs and alcohol, as well as avoiding confrontation, that others measured their reform and claimed it a success. These were the only behaviours they *could* change while incarcerated, and most seemed to feel that if they could achieve this, they could also desist from crime and substance abuse on the outside.

Secondly, some of those who spoke at length about how they had changed in prison (like Dan, who ascribed such power to having time to think) nevertheless did not feel confident they would act differently upon release. Conversely, some of those who did not describe any mechanism by which they might have been rehabilitated did feel they had changed their ways for good. This was made possible by the commonly held view that change had to originate within the self (see also Crewe, 2009) and that sometimes all that was necessary was an internal change, which could be achieved in a moment. Research has endorsed the notion that such 'critical moments' can provide a catalyst for desistance (MacDonald, Webster, Shildrick and Simpson, 2011). Often the motivation to change was provided by the interaction with a loved one, usually a child.

> Me and my daughter are very, very close. Eehm, and my daughter had said ... 'I don't need a dad in the jail, I need a dad out here'. ... and that really gave me a heavy guilt trip. Cause, although I've kind of skirted by that thought, I didn't actually think about it in any deep, deep way. But when she's actually saying it to me it kinda it, it (.) hurt me, I could feel it in my heart and I'm saying to myself 'she's absolutely right'. (Lino)

In Lino, Tony, Tim and Jack's accounts (who were all on licence) this type of instant personal change was most important. This goes beyond

Comfort's (2008) concept of 'as if' reform, because these men did not refer to aspects of their prison experience that reformed them. Any engagement with services was seen as a tool they used in their *self*-initiated project of change and was positioned as a marker rather than as a driver of reform and rehabilitation.

> it's been me that's changed it, you know what I mean. It's been me that's done it, but, like there's the social work, there's this, there's that, I've went to them and communicated with them and if there had been a course or whatever to do, I've put myself forward for it, whereas before I didn't, I just went 'get away from me'. (Jack)

Because they did not attribute their reform to their imprisonment, they tended to be negative about the impact of their prison sentence and see it as having failed in its purpose of reform. Jack, for example, said that 'ah' they years that I've spent in prison (.) not done me any good'.

Some of the men's accounts, though, made it clear that they felt that reform had been achieved. They said they were glad they got caught, that it was the best thing that could have happened and that their sentence changed things for the better, and usually credited aspects of their imprisonment with a significant part of their reform. This was the case for Colin, Gordon, James, Peter (for part of his account), who were all at the end of their sentence, and Andy who was on licence. Most of their views have already been described: Gordon attributed his change (partly) to cognitive behavioural courses (but also to a large extent to his own efforts), James to the amount of time he had had to think, Colin to the interest taken by staff, and Andy to his subjection to discipline and going to the gym. Colin and Andy offered an especially passive account of reform where undergoing imprisonment had changed them, without much agency needed. For them, then, prison had achieved its purpose of reform.

Others felt that prison had not achieved reform, but that they would nevertheless desist from offending. Neil, Alex (both at the end of their sentences) and Mohammed (on licence) all talked about having matured and grown older, and therefore having changed. Similarly, Smitty (on licence) felt that it was unlikely he would reoffend, not because he had changed but because the world outside had, with his friends no longer pursuing criminal activities. These interviewees did not attribute change to any feature of their imprisonment except for time passing, and therefore did not see this as an achievement of purpose.

> I can just feel, now, that eehm, that, that my willingness or propensity to commit similar crimes in the future would be really low, you

know, really low ... I don't view it in moral terms. I'm still (.) criminally minded, I still, I don't think have too much scruples that way. (Alex)

Finally, there were those who felt that they would return to offending (or were at risk of doing so) and that imprisonment had failed in its aim of reform.

I think I deserved what I got, but while I was in there I do think it could have been handled differently ... the content was abysmal. (Stephen)

Despite the proliferation of critical views about reform, in most of the men's accounts it was not a failure of reform that they thought would be their downfall, but a lack of rehabilitation.

Rehabilitation

Rex expressed the concept of rehabilitation as 'helping them with problems behind their offending' (2005, p. 86), but in the interviews with those at the end of their sentence, discussions around rehabilitation often focused on being prepared for release in such a way that they would be able to deal with the world outside.

I've got a right struggle with/ I don't even know where I'm going or where I'm going get a flat from or anything like that, this is all things I think about just now. (Doug)

While this often did not constitute help with problems that had led to their original offence (for example Doug had not been homeless when he committed his crime), the interviewees did worry that the circumstances they had to face once outside would lead to further offending.

But, I've told them this, see, if I can get a place, a place of my own, I can get my girl at weekends, you know, but they just keep on putting me in the frying pan (.) back into the street and that's not going to help. In here (.) I'm getting out in couple of weeks and I've not got anywhere to go. So I know what's going to happen, you know what I mean. (Graham)

Worries about accommodation were the most common, especially for those who were returning to Glasgow, where accommodation for prisoners upon release is recognised to be scarce and of a poor standard

(Loucks, 2007). Most expected to be housed in a hostel, which they saw as a real obstacle to desistance:

> I don't see the point of going into a hostel, where there's drug abusers in hostels...eehm, is one of them going to try to pull a set of tools out on me, to rob me, because if I feel that, I will end up carrying a knife myself and I'd rather just stab one straight away. See, like that, but that's putting me in a position, because of my history and I'll be back inside. (Ian)

On the topic of preparation for release, my recruitment strategy with those at the end of their sentence is likely to have had a significant impact. Because I was interviewing men who were soon to be released from a closed prison, rather than an open prison, I was selecting those who had either not been transferred to the open estate, or who had transferred and for various reasons been returned to the closed prison. Accordingly, they were usually not offered parole before their final possible release date.

Many of those who had not been to the open estate blamed their lack of progression on delays in the system, for example reports on courses they had attended not being completed on time.

> I done a course, eh control and anger regulating emotions course (.) and after I done that it took them five months to get me the report for my course and I couldn't move onto Castle Huntly without that. (Doug)

In their lack of progression to – and/or (for some) their return from – the open estate, procedural (in)justice (Jackson et al., 2010; Tyler, 1990, 1997, 2010) played a large role in the men's perceptions. Within the prison environment, procedural justice has been conceptualised as having four determinants: voice (whether the prisoner has any input in decisions that concern him), neutrality (whether decisions are made consistently, rather than capriciously), treatment with respect and dignity, and trust that the authorities sincerely want to do what is right (Jackson et al., 2010, p. 5). As Doug's quote above illustrates, the men often did not feel that their wellbeing was taken into consideration, that they were treated with respect, or that the authorities were concerned with doing what was right for them. Having a voice was also an issue: while relationships with staff were generally cordial, there was much tension evident in the negotiation of progression and release, a process in which prisoners felt without voice. The men saw themselves as powerless; all they could do was jump through the hoops before them, and as already noted in relation to cognitive behavioural courses, even this did not guarantee progression. Consequently, several of the men, like Ian, had decided to not even try:

> I don't ask for parole, you know what I'm talking about? I've never asked for parole, in any of my sentences. Because it all comes down to, the way your parole is, is this man likely to reoffend in the time he's on parole.…So, even if you want to jump through hoops for them, they'll probably still not give you it, so I just say, fuck them, I'll just do my time. (Ian)

The sense of injustice was strongest for Robert, who had been to the open estate but had been returned and refused parole on the word of his ex-wife. His account largely revolved around this and other instances of perceived procedural injustice he, disabled and unwell, had experienced within the prison.

> I got (.) refused parole, I was at an open prison and on the word of a, what I would call a malicious female, I was downgraded. Back to here, without (.) I have no recall on it, all I can do is put on a bit of paper (.) but it goes to deaf ears, they're not interested. It's like, people go out on parole and if someone doesn't like you, they lift the phone and you're back without any (.) it doesn't matter.

Prisoners who have successfully progressed and who are released from an open prison are likely to be more positive about their preparation for release than this group of prisoners. Furthermore, at other times in their sentence these men, too, might have focused on other aspects of rehabilitation and been more positive than with release looming large and worries over their uncertain future therefore dominant.

The SPS's 'offender outcomes' (2011) mention several different foci of rehabilitation besides accommodation. These include mental and physical health, substance abuse, employability, literacy and relationships. It was in relation to substance abuse and employability that the interviewees most often mentioned having benefited from their imprisonment. Problems with drugs and alcohol were seen as playing a big part in the causation of offending by many of the men.

> I never, ever, ever committed my offences sober, never, nah never, I've never/ I don't even think I've ever been done sober. No, if I get

a drink in me I'm different, completely different, you know what I mean? (Jack)

However, the prison was not often credited with a purposeful intervention; instead it was their own motivation, sometimes combined with the high cost of drugs in prison, which some of the men felt meant that they were able to tackle their addiction problems in prison. Several used the fact that they had refrained from using drugs to imbue their prison sentence with positive meaning:

But I think I was glad to get away from that, away from the drugs, I think (.) eh at the time/ well, I was thinking that's the only way I could have broke this drugs cycle. (Tony)

For these men drug-related rehabilitation was one of the purposes of their imprisonment, but one that originated with them, rather than intended by the powers that be. Others, however, said that prison had had the opposite effect and they had started taking drugs and had acquired a habit in order to deal with the pains of imprisonment, especially at the very start of their sentence.

A lot of people use drugs, mostly heroin because it's out of your system very quickly. And every one of them were using it, so I was straight into that environment and that's where I was introduced to it basically. (Mohammed)

In relation to education and employment training, while many had undertaken this, they tended not to see this as rehabilitation, but pursued it for its own sake.

Aye, I got an O level in English and, oh, I was happy as a lark, you know what I mean. I had never achieved anything like that in my life. (Stephen)

Although many of the men had never worked, those who were still in prison did not often mention this as one of the main problems in their lives. For most of those on licence, however, not being able to find employment was a major problem (see Chapter 5). This illustrates the different level of rehabilitation necessary at different times in the sentence.

Cause like the last year I've been out and I've maybe been sitting in the house and I'm pissed off and I'm fed up with everything, can't get a job, you feel as if nothing's going right for yea. I just/ I've had me sitting saying to myself 'I feel like being back in the jail the now'. (Jack)

Given the difficulties of finding a job with a long-term prison sentence on their criminal record, none of the men mentioned the training they had had in prison as achieving its aim of increasing employability prospects. In relation to the other offender-related outcomes very little was said, except that contact with family and friends was minimal, often as a conscious strategy on the part of the prisoner (see Chapter 4), a situation in which the prison appeared to do little to intervene.

This section has examined rehabilitation efforts made while the men were still imprisoned. Those on licence also had much to say about their rehabilitation *after* they were released, but as this ties in closely with the shape of their narratives compared to those in prison, these views are discussed in Chapters 4 and 5. Suffice it to say here that, even though they were overwhelmingly positive about the efforts of their criminal justice social workers, they nonetheless often felt that their rehabilitation had failed because of their institutionalisation, financial strains and the impossibility of finding employment with a criminal record in the present economic climate.

Deterrence

Deterrence can work in two ways. General deterrence refers to the fear of punishment instilled in the general public by criminal sentencing; in this context, because someone is sent to prison for a certain crime, those contemplating a similar crime might refrain from offending. This was expressed by Rex as 'show other people that they won't get away with crime' (2005, p. 85). Special or individual deterrence is the fear of punishment that might keep current (or past) prisoners from offending in the future, expressed by Rex in her research as 'show them that crime does not pay' (2005, p. 85). Unsurprisingly, the men I interviewed spoke at much greater length about the deterrent effect their punishment had on them or their compatriots, than on the effect of the sentence on the public at large. Therefore, general deterrence is only discussed very briefly before a more in-depth look at individual deterrence.

General deterrence was mentioned in passing by three of the men, all of whom commented that their sentence had been (or had to be) an example to others. For example, Lino said:

that ten year sentence, although it was very difficult to handle, at the end of the day what other option did they have or the court have?

> If the court would have just let me walk that would have been like 'it's alright to do this type of thing'. If they gave me a small sentence people would have went 'oh I'll do that as well, I'm no bothered, the jail's no that bad'.

As the nature of general deterrence is that it works on people other than the person punished, they had no further insights to offer on this aim of sentencing. However, Malcolm did comment on the role the media played in disseminating the message, after saying that the judge had made an example of him:

> there was quite a lot about it in the paper, basically ken? It just said if anybody's gonna step into Mr X's shoes, be warned that you will face big sentences, blah, blah, blah, ken?

This highlights that for general deterrence to be achieved, the general public needs to know about the sentence. None of the three men were especially opposed to this aim of sentencing.

With regards to individual deterrence, there was an uneasy mix of views and opinions amongst the participants on whether imprisonment was a deterrent to future criminal behaviour. A recurrent theme was that prison was too easy to deter people, and many mentioned TVs, DVD players and PlayStations as examples of the overly comfortable nature of the modern prison experience (see also Crewe, 2009, p. 430; Halsey, 2007). They felt that conditions inside should be more difficult in order to make people keener to avoid further sentences.

> It doesn't do nothing to you. That's what I'm saying to you, it doesn't bother me if they want to put me in jail, in fact I'll spare you the breath and I'll go myself [both laugh] ... I'm only not going be doing it [stop offending] through my choice, do you know what I mean, through me, not because there's a prison there saying 'oh you'll be comin' here'. [Laughs] 'So fuckin' what', know what I mean, you don't frighten me with your prison. (Jack)

Short sentences in particular were seen as an easy option, and as being no deterrent. Interviewees spoke of having had many such sentences in the past, without any effect, and some had used them in the past as a respite from their problems outside.

> I had a drug habit and I was getting too messed up, I used to deliberately get prison sentences, just to get off the drugs, you know, just go

away for a couple of month an get off the drugs. But it's that easy, you know what I mean. (Smitty)

Yet, at the same time, short-term sentences were often portrayed as more difficult to cope with, as the men felt it was much harder to limit their horizons (see Chapter 4) with a release date relatively close.

While most respondents did not think the prison was successful in deterring people from crime, their disapproval of the current, easy, conditions in prison (whether genuine or not) made it clear that they thought it *should*. Deterrence was seen as a legitimate aim of their sentence. This is in line with Rex's finding (2005) that offenders saw prison sentences as aimed mostly at retribution and deterrence. Accordingly, the theme of deterrence often arose spontaneously in the participants' accounts, as did rehabilitation, while other purposes were often only considered in response to my questions. Jack was talking about his early life when he said:

I think, the first time I ever went to court I got my detentions, do you know what I mean (.) I don't think that was right. I think maybe if I'd have had got something that wasn't the jail but it was a fright, that maybe have changed me. But it never, I was right to jail so the fear of going to prison was knocked out of me right away, you know what I mean.

Jack wished he had been deterred earlier in his criminal career, and his quote highlights the possibility that prison could be more effective as a symbolic deterrent for those who have not yet experienced it than for those who have been there and managed to adapt to prison conditions (as everyone who goes to prison must to some extent). This was supported by Alex, who said of his first sentence:

I'd rather not have been in prison, because everybody would rather be free, but once I got to the tail end of it and I was released and I looked back and I went 'you know, that wasn't so bad, that wasn't the end of the world there, you know'.

Large-scale quantitative research has also found that greater experience of imprisonment can diminish its deterrent effect (Drago, Galbiati and Vertova, 2009). This has been explained with reference to exposure to criminal influences, or finding conditions better than expected (Nagin, Cullen and Jonson, 2009), but the current findings suggest that it may also be a result of adaptation and institutionalisation.

Those who were the most disparaging about the deterrent effect of imprisonment were either at the end of their sentence or on licence.[2] Those on licence who felt most strongly that the conditions in prison should be more adverse were those who also acknowledged their own institutionalisation (see also Chapter 4). For them, prison had become 'a second home' (Jack) and even a retreat from what were often difficult lives on the outside.

> A lot of people I talk to say I'm institutionalised, eh (.) and in there you've no worries, you don't need to worry about a wife or a partner or. Just, I enjoyed it and I didn't want to come out. (Tony)

While interviewees maintained that they would have been deterred more by harsher prison conditions, these statements highlight the tension between the inevitable adaptation to sentences and deterrence (as also noted by Farrall and Calverley, 2006).

On the other hand, several of the interviewees said that one of their motivations to stay away from crime was to avoid further imprisonment. For some, the gain was just not worth the pain. Neil, for example, felt he had not made enough money in the drug trade to make his years in prison worthwhile.

> Basically, for the amount of years I have spent in the jail, it's really, it's a mug's game, it's a pure mug's game, the amount of years you are having to spend in prison for the amount of money that you make. (Neil)

These considerations, though, did not necessarily mean that these men were confident that their sentence would actually deter them from future offending.

> Well, getting a sentence itself is, the sentence is meant to deter you not to do it again. But there's myself as an example. The first sentence couldn't have deterred me not to do it again, I done it again, I done it again, I done it again. (Neil)

A stronger deterrent for some respondents was the prospect that, given their record, they would receive longer and longer sentences in the future, which they wanted to avoid. Similarly, for some of those still on licence, this was also an effective deterrent, as they would have to serve the rest of their original sentence (or an indeterminate sentence, for those on life licence) as well as any new sentence.

To me (.) prison's no deterrent. The only deterrent for me is my licence hanging over my head and I can lose everything I've had a taste of what could get took away. (Tim)

Age also seemed to play a role in how the interviewees thought about imprisonment; the older they were, the more heavily the prospect of more years spent in prison weighed.

Prison is not HARD. It's only when you realise you've missed out on life. Eeh, my time is more valuable now than it was, say, twenty year ago. Now I'm an old man and every year is/ but you don't think about how long you've got left when you're in your twenties or thirties, but once you reach/ I'm 69 now, once you reach my age, you realise you're living on borrowed time. (Dan)

Some prisoners made a distinction between the conditions *inside* prison, which they felt were easy to cope with, and the overall *effects* of imprisonment, such as being away from family and the world moving on without you, which meant they did not want to return.

It's hard to sort of sum it up, but (.) eh I certainly don't want to be doing another sentence like that, no, although it wasn't hard or anything like that. It was easier to get my head down about it, know what I mean, than it is the shorter sentences. But eh, just (.) things change too much when you're in for long terms, know what I mean, and it's getting back out and trying to fit into the community where everything's changed, know what I mean, it's a bit harder, know what I mean? (Smitty)

It is notable that even those who endorsed the deterrent effect of imprisonment in the quotes above also still emphasised that they did not find it difficult to live in prison. Tim said prison itself is not a deterrent, and both Dan and Smitty said that prison is not hard before going onto explain why they did not want to return.

The interviewees' apparent need to qualify their aversion to prison and the fact that the notion that 'prison is easy' was expressed so widely raises the possibility that, being imprisoned *men*, they did not want to admit to weakness or emotional difficulty. Having to be tough and autonomous and avoiding emotion are all elements of the dominant way of performing masculinity, or hegemonic masculinity, in the West (Connell, 1996; Garde, 2003; Pollack, 1995; Vincent, 2006) and such elements form a code especially likely to be adhered to by working class young men who cannot rely on having power within the workplace to achieve masculinity (Evans and Wallace, 2008). Prisons in particular provide a stronghold for hegemonic masculinity, with violence valorised (Evans and Wallace, 2008), and the prisoner code dictates that male prisoners do not admit to fear and 'suffer in silence', even when they are not coping (Sabo, Kupers and London, 2001, p. 10). Although not all prisoners will subscribe to the view that this is what it takes to be a man, even those who think it is acceptable to display emotion are unlikely to share their emotions with other prisoners, and being 'tough' is very much part of the 'overarching story about how one must act in prison' (Evans and Wallace, 2008, p. 498). Several influential prison studies have noted that it is those who bear their sentence with (apparent) equanimity who are the most admired (Crewe, 2009; Sykes, 1958). This might explain why Tim credited his licence with being a deterrent but not prison, even though licence logically relies on imprisonment to deter people. This way he was able to maintain the guise of a 'real man' (Sykes, 1958, p. 102), because there is not likely to be a similar macho culture (nor a notional fellow-prisoner audience) about the endurance of licence.

Other men still commented on the rather favourable conditions, but also integrated this with the real pain they felt during their imprisonment, because of what it meant to be imprisoned.

> I think it was the length of the sentence for a start that really hurt me like, cause I hear a lot of people saying that the jail's like a holiday camp and that, so I mean, and it's (.) it is true, I found that myself when I was in there it is/ there's a lot of luxuries, a lot of comforts, a lot of home comforts, like at the end of the day it's (.) and that's another cliché you hear, it's (.) it's the being locked away and that's the truth really, do you know what I mean, it really hurts. Well, it really hurt me badly, do you know what I mean? (Andy)

The finding that emerges is that some prisoners no longer see prison as painful, because they have adapted to its conditions, and therefore they no longer experience it as a deterrent – rather, they experience it as a retreat. However, this seems to be connected to institutionalisation and problems adapting to freedom upon release (see Chapter 4). The group discourse amongst prisoners that prison is easy may also have masked, to some extent, any deterrent meaning it had for the men. Deterrence furthermore appears to depend on a subtle process influenced by timing. For some of the men, sentences may have been too long to deter, because they inevitably adapted. However, the relevance of age means that there may come a point, despite this adaptation, where people have 'had enough' and want more out of life. This suggests that sometimes it is not the painfulness of prison but the feeling that 'real life' happens outside that leads to deterrence. On the other hand, some men found (or admitted) that imprisonment was painful in itself and enough reason to try to stay away in the future.

Retribution or punishment

The word retribution was used only once by one of the interviewees, when Alex said about the purpose of imprisonment: 'I suppose you could say that there's a kind of punishment, eeh (.) societal retribution'. All the others, when discussing how their sentence was supposed to make them suffer, simply called this punishment. Sexton (2007) has examined the punishment inherent in the prison experience in great detail and found that while imprisonment was largely seen as punitive as a whole, many features of day-to-day life in prison were also experienced as punishment, such as amenities that were broken or withheld, the pettiness and inconsistencies of rules, and the many ways in which life in prison was different and removed from life outside. Her research project, however, took punishment as its starting point for the exploration of 'penal consciousness', or what punishment is in the experiences of the punished and she did note that most of her respondents did not bring up the concept of punishment spontaneously, but only in response to her questions. In the research described here, mentions of punishment were also relatively rare: punishment was only mentioned as a purpose by fourteen of the men, and then usually only briefly. This is interesting in light of Rex's finding (2005) that retribution, which she operationalised as 'make them pay for what they did wrong' (p. 82), was the purpose of imprisonment most commonly selected by offenders, but also the most unpopular aim, with only 40 per cent of her offender participants agreeing this *should* be an aim of the court.

The way in which the men talked about being punished was very similar to their statements about deterrence. Discussions of punishment also centred on prison being too easy to achieve its aim.

> PAUL: To be honest with you, it's pretty cushy in here, compared to what it should be.
> MS: How, what do you think it should be?
> PAUL: A lot harder, let's put it that way, you know, it's a punishment. It's not walking about and classes and sweeping floors and stuff like that.

The lack of distinction between deterrence and punishment in the men's accounts is telling. In the philosophy of punishment they are clearly distinct. Deterrence is justified through a consequentialist, utilitarian logic; its intended outcome is a reduction in crime. Retribution, by contrast, draws on a deontological logic; it is seen as being justified in itself as an inherently proper response to crime. However, when experiencing a sentence this distinction will be difficult to perceive, unless the purpose of the sentence has been made explicit. The interviewees recognised that both deterrence and punishment rely on inflicted pain, which meant that for them the main difference between deterrence and punishment was whether imprisonment was likely to make them stop offending, in which case its purpose was deterrence. If not, punishment seemed to function as a kind of back-up purpose: if their sentence had failed to deter them, they were still being punished (despite their portrayal of prison conditions as 'easy'). Neil noted that the judge had said he would never learn his lesson and thought that therefore his sentence could not have been meant as a deterrent. He said:

> If it's not a deterrent, I don't know what it is. A punishment, if it's not a deterrent, that's what, they'll punish you for it.

In this, the interviewees' view of their punishment mirrors the state's retreat from the more ambitious welfarist approach, with its aim to reduce crime rates, towards a 'just deserts' approach, which only has to deliver punishment to succeed (Garland, 1996).

Despite the lack of distinction between deterrence and punishment, there were subtle differences in the way the two purposes were discussed. Punishment was less desired than deterrence as a purpose, as it did not have any positive consequences for the men themselves. While they often expressed the wish that they had been deterred earlier in their criminal careers and hoped that this sentence would do the trick, they did not feel the same way about punishment. In addition, punishment was a more salient purpose for those at the start of their sentence than deterrence, which was little mentioned by this group, perhaps because they were so far away from release. In addition, loss of freedom figured much more heavily in the discussions of punishment than in those of deterrence.

> But (.) the punishment for me is taking that away, that liberty, that's the biggest punishment for me. My girlfriend has just been on holiday and we were supposed to be there together and that really hurt, not being there. (David)

This may reflect a change in emphasis in the prison service's message to prisoners, with loss of liberty being the punishment, rather than conditions inside.

> See, the way I seen prisons was, before, when you got sentenced it was more for the punishment, eh? Like way back in the Y[oung] O[ffenders Institute]s and that. When the officers used to like really come down hard on you. Back then, when you got jail it was meant to be for punishment, you were PUNISHED inside. But now, when you get the jail, it is only to take your freedom away. (Colin)

Other than these differences, the pains of imprisonment described under the heading of punishment were very similar to those described as deterrents: the world moving on without you and the pain of being locked in. It is notable that, even though the men were not as supportive of punishment as they were of deterrence (and rehabilitation) they did not reject it as a proper purpose of their sentence. In fact, several said they deserved some form of punishment.

Incapacitation

Incapacitation was by far the least developed of the purposes of imprisonment in the interviews. Twelve of the men mentioned incapacitation, but it did not play a large role in their accounts; they generally just said this might have been part of the point of their imprisonment. This is not surprising, as incapacitation is what happens while imprisonment takes place; it does not have to be achieved through separate means (whereas even punishment requires adverse conditions) and it has no implications for prisoners' futures, as it ends with release. Rex's layman's definition of incapacitation is 'keep them away from offending' (2005, p. 85). The only way the interviewees could deny that this was achieved was through either maintaining that they would not have offended if they had been free during the period of their imprisonment, or by disclosing offences during their imprisonment (see Wood, Williams and James, 2010). While some of the interviewees (especially those who were imprisoned for their first offence) would have been able to claim the former, they did not mention incapacitation. Those who did tended to agree that they should be incapacitated:

> I think my sentence at the time did achieve its purpose, they just wanted me off the street at the time, cause AT THE TIME I was very dangerous. (Stephen)

Only Colin, who was otherwise very supportive of his imprisonment, expressed himself in such a way that opposition to this point of view is suggested:

> MS: And what do you think the point was of sending you to prison at that time?
>
> COLIN: At that time? Because I was-, *no, in their eyes* I suppose I was a danger to the public selling drugs (emphasis added).

He starts to say that he was a danger, but changes his mind and suggests that it was (only?) in the eyes of those who sentenced him that he was dangerous. Others did not evaluate whether they should have been incapacitated, but merely reported this purpose because the judge had mentioned it:

> That was in the judge's report, basically if I'm locked away then the public has less chance of getting harmed. (Gordon)

These findings suggest that incapacitation only becomes salient as a purpose when either the prisoner perceives himself as dangerous or it is explicitly mentioned as a purpose by the court. The fact that there was little mention of, but also little opposition to the aim of incapacitation, might be due to the fact that those to whose situation it did not readily apply did not think of it as an aim of their sentence.

Other purposes

The above discussion reveals, in considerable detail, how and to what extent justifications of punishment were expressed in the interviewees' accounts. However, some of the men I spoke to also mentioned different purposes, which tended to be far more benign and individual than the aims of punishment already discussed. Several of the men made statements at some point in their interview which implied that they believed that there was some larger plan for their lives and that their imprisonment had played an important role in this. In Chris' case, this was made quite explicit in the following exchange:

> CHRIS: The purpose, this has been thrown at me at this time in my life yeah, because of my age and to get eehm/ to start a fresh start, that's what I think [laughs].
>
> MS: Do you think that's what the judge was thinking?

CHRIS: No that isn't what the judge was thinking, that's what the/
MS: /The Universe was thinking?/
CHRIS: /whoever, the Almighty, was thinking.

Several others believed that their imprisonment had kept them from some greater harm on the outside: Lino avoided the smack epidemic that hit his town a year after he entered prison, which he felt would have led to him overdosing. Tim felt imprisonment had saved him from himself:

Keep me alive [short laugh], it's kept me alive, it's kept me (.) it's kept me here. I guess it's (.) I've spoken to people that knew me from then and girlfriends that knew me then and they've told me as well, 'you were going down a path of destruction and you're a better man for it now' so.

For others, the prison was a more conscious place of retreat from the world. They had usually spent a lot of time in institutions, whether prison or children's homes, and therefore found life inside easier.

IAN: I'm that used to being in here myself, no pressure, with no pressure, no hassle, and then going out with a wean screaming all the time. You know what I'm talking about, it's just (.).
MS: So has prison sort of become normal life for you?
IAN: Aye. It's easy isn't it? You know where you stand don't you?
MS: So what is the meaning of a prison sentence for you now then?
IAN: It's (.) you commit a crime, init, they have to take you off the streets, don't they?
MS: But I mean for you personally, what does it mean for you?
IAN: A break, sometimes. (.)

Thereby the punishment had become a resource for Ian and others; some respite from the chaotic and unpredictable world outside. Issues of institutionalisation are discussed in greater depth in Chapter 4, but it is telling that the way in which these men saw prison meant that for them, it no longer needed a purpose or justification, because they were comfortable with it, preferring it to freedom at times.

Conclusion

It is unsurprising that in a narrative context the purposes that have relevance for the men beyond their imprisonment (deterrence and reform/ rehabilitation) have much more salience than those that do not. These purposes, and especially reform and rehabilitation, allow prisoners to believe in change and to construct a story in which their imprisonment is cast in a positive light (Comfort, 2008), whereas retribution and incapacitation do not provide any fulcrum for change beyond the period of imprisonment. The need for a positive narrative and its impact on the meaning of imprisonment is discussed in much greater depth in Chapter 4. The finding that the interviewees were especially fervent in their wish for rehabilitation and reform, and accordingly very critical of the way in which the prison pursued these aims, also confirms other findings that these tend to be the preferred aims of sentences for prisoners and offenders (Ashkar and Kenny, 2008; Comfort, 2008; Halsey, 2007; Liebling et al., 2011; Rex, 2005). Where my findings and previous research findings depart is in the association between positive staff–prisoner relationships and prisoners seeing their sentence as rehabilitative (Patrick and Marsh, 2001; Sparks et al., 1996). Despite the relationships between prisoners and staff in the research prison being good by all accounts, the men I interviewed at the end of their sentence very rarely saw this as contributing to the rehabilitative impact of their sentence. To achieve such impact, more individual attention would have been needed. While more negative prisoner–staff relationships would most likely have led to more negative accounts of imprisonment overall, research by Liebling et al. (2011) suggests that views on rehabilitation can be very similar under regimes where relationships with staff are much less positive.

It is notable that the men did not object to efforts to change them motivated by a late-modern rehabilitation agenda, in which the offender's welfare is overshadowed by the need to (be seen to) protect the public (McNeill, 2012; Robinson, 2008). Rather, they welcomed a focus of rehabilitative efforts on their offending behaviour and did not make a distinction according to the motivation for this focus. In their accounts, any reduction in offending or concomitant change in character they could achieve would automatically also benefit them and their families, making it thereby impossible for such interventions to ignore their welfare, no matter whether the intention was to help them or to benefit others. However, many felt that managerialist methods and approaches meant that they had, in fact, *not* been helped to move away from offending and that therefore the prison had neither managed to reduce harm to others nor to benefit them personally. It was not the motivation behind rehabilitative and reformative efforts they objected to, but the way the prison regime pursued these, and failed to achieve them.

Their contention that prison does not deter because it is too easy was likely influenced by the need to perform masculinity and a positive prison role, but also highlighted that when one is forced to adapt to an environment for a long period of time, that environment is unlikely to hold the same fear in the future. This was even more vividly illustrated by some of the men preferring the prison environment to the outside world, which highlights the danger of long-term institutionalisation in the absence of meaningful individual support.

In terms of their future prospects of desistance, the majority of the men felt that the prison had not contributed to a reduction in their motivation (or need) to offend. Some felt that they had reformed themselves, or had matured, and therefore were less likely to offend in the future. The way these men described their personal change suggested that it would have happened with or without their imprisonment; it either hinged on a moment of insight (often stimulated by interactions with family) or depended on mere time passing. Others did not see themselves as reformed and were resigned to further offending in the future. Only a minority of men gave the prison (some of the) credit for their reform. They said that they were grateful for their sentence, because it had made all the difference. Chapter 5 will examine their accounts in-depth and question what role interventions by the regime really played in their reform. On the whole, though, there is little in this chapter to suggest that imprisonment, as it stands, contributes much to the desistance process of most prisoners.

4
Legitimacy and the Impact of the Prison Environment

Introduction

The previous chapter examined to what extent normative purposes of punishment found expression in the men's accounts, using an 'etic' level of analysis. This chapter focuses more closely on the men's narratives, and the meanings of imprisonment contained within them, by examining how the men came to see their sentence as (un)fair. As not much in-depth work has been completed on offenders' views of the legitimacy of their sentence, I draw on concepts from work in other areas, including Bottoms' work on compliance with community penalties (2001), Beetham's theory of the legitimacy of political power relations (1991) and research on prisoners' views of the prison regime (Carrabine, 2004; Sparks et al., 1996).

In the discussion of issues of legitimacy in this chapter, it is clear that the prison environment had a major impact on the views held by the men. Therefore, this chapter will have a bifurcated structure and for the first time in this book will consider different groups of interviewees in turn. First, it will discuss the bases on which all the interviewees evaluated their sentence. Then, it will focus solely on those at the end of their sentence for some sections, because the prison environment was still actively working upon them. It will then explore how the views of the men on licence differed, and how the prison environment still impacted on their lives, before returning to the implications for the notion of legitimacy in sentencing.

Evaluating the sentence

The men I spoke to used various measures against which to evaluate their sentence, including their own expectations, consistency with others' sentences, the court's standing to judge, their culpability or guilt and the level of harm they had caused. In line with earlier research (Casper et al., 1988; McGinnis and Carlson, 1981), negative perceptions were often related to the sentence being longer than expected. Expectations were based on previous personal experience with the criminal justice system and feedback from others, often lawyers (see also Casper et al., 1988; McGinnis and Carlson, 1981).

> I was gutted ken. I didn't think I was getting that long cause I was only caught with 4.3 grams, it wasn't a lot ken? Eeh, I was pretty stunned actually, I didn't think I'd get that long. My lawyer told me, right, maybe four, five, I didn't think I'd get six year three months, so. (Malcolm)

> I knew four years is a long term sentence, I knew I was getting a long term sentence but four years is the least, so I was jumpin' for joy when he said that and then I didn't really care what he said for the extended sentence, I think he said 'four year extended sentence', but I was just happy with the four year, eh, it was a result and a half you know what I mean so, it was quite a lenient sentence for what I done. (Doug)

Malcolm's phrase 'I was pretty stunned' and Doug's 'jumping for joy' illustrate how expectations had the greatest impact on the men's reaction immediately following sentencing, in both a positive and negative direction.

Another known contributory factor to feelings of injustice is perceived inconsistency in sentencing (Casper et al., 1988; Casper, 1972; Indermaur, 1994). This seemed to affect the interviewees' perspective mostly after sentencing – usually when they learned of other prisoners' sentences for similar or worse offences.

> I think it is a joke. Because, I've seen guys/ there's not a structure, there's not a set sentence. If one person does a murder they get nine years, another person does a murder, they get twenty years. It should be a set sentence or a set tariff. I don't know, there's guys in here for murder that's doing a shorter time than me. And I'm in for attempted murder. So you're like that 'where is the justice system in that?' (Gordon)

When sentences were shorter than expected or than would be consistent with the sentences of others, this was unsurprisingly met with relief and acceptance, rather than a sense of injustice.

> I was expecting not to get back out. Because I was told the last time before I get another LTP [long-term prison sentence], I would get a life one. So the seven, it was like that, cool. It was still big, but there was still hope. (Ian)

There is so much at stake for the prisoner receiving a long-term prison sentence that it is unsurprising that the men I interviewed did not morally oppose sentencing decisions that they perceived as being in their favour. There were a few who commented that their sentence should have been longer, and that their actual sentence therefore was unfair, but this was not accompanied by a sense of injustice.

> SMITTY: I could have stopped and helped and stuff like that, know what I mean, but eh (.) aye I suppose it wasn't a fair sentence, I should have got more than I did for it.
> MS: What do you think you should have gotten?
> SMITTY: Well, everybody I know that's been done with death by dangerous driving's got seven year, AT LEAST, you know, and that's what I thought I would have got, at least seven year. So when they said two and a half year I was like that 'wow', know what I mean.

The men who were pleasantly surprised at the length of their sentence accepted it for instrumental, rather than normative reasons. Within their interviews there were few contradictions or complaints about the criminal justice system. Casper also found that a 'fair' sentence meant largely two things to his interviewees: '(1) a good deal – something less than they might have gotten; (2.) the going rate for an offence.' (1972, p. 89). The men I interviewed who felt they had had 'a good deal' or perceived their sentence as consistent with those of others very seldom complained about their sentence.

In modern penality, it is not only the length of the prison sentence imposed by the judge that can be perceived as inconsistent. Alan felt that it was highly unfair that he was not only imprisoned, but also prosecuted under the Proceeds of Crime Act, given that this did not happen to most offenders convicted of similar offences of petty drug dealing.

> ALAN: But eehm, like that first time I was in (.) eehm, I was in with guys that had been done with kilos of the stuff and not ONE of them had proceeds of crime, and I got done with such a little bit. Because basically, they had nothing to go for, they had no/ you

> know what I mean, they had no house, they had never worked all
> their life, they had no house, they were...
> MS: Yeah, they were like drug addicts themselves?
> ALAN: ...yeah, and it was like, the system was going to punish me
> because I worked all my life, had a good job, I paid my taxes, so I
> SHOULD HAVE known better, that's how I felt it was.

In effect, Alan felt he was being doubly punished because he had made
something of his life, despite by his account having profited very little
from dealing drugs. For him, it was a combination of inconsistency
and disagreement about the facts of the case that rankled. In another
instance of inconsistency, Stephen felt that, while his life sentence had
been fair, the number of years he actually spent in prison before being
released on licence had been unfair and inconsistent.

> Well, because I did kill the man, I did deserve life but (.) going by
> what I said to you earlier about people doing less time than me, I
> don't think I should have done as long. I should have done less, I was
> a Trustee for 12 years, 13 years. I didn't give them any hassle, they
> had no reason really to hold me so long.

Stephen felt that his behaviour had given the prison authorities no
reason to keep him incarcerated for almost 20 years.

Many of the interviewees saw the harm they had inflicted as justifying
their sentence.

> Drugs is (.) it's the scourge of society, it is and I'm ashamed to say that
> I was partly involved/ fair enough naively but I was still part of it and
> that's why I deserve my sentence, you know, even though I was being
> used, I still was involved in it. (Robert)

> If I was the judge I might have sentenced me to a bit longer actually,
> to be honest, because I'm/ you've got to look at the/ the guy was
> stabbed like 13 times or something do you know what I mean, in his
> heart an all that nearly. (Andy)

Despite little official communication about the moral link between
crime and punishment (see Schinkel, in press-a), some men *did* reflect
on this, more or less of their own accord. They evaluated their sentence
along normative lines and felt that it had been just. However, when the
interviewees felt that they had *not* caused much harm, they often still
agreed with their sentence on more formal grounds.

JAMES: I think alcohol is more dangerous than cannabis definitely.

MS: So do you think, if you look at it that way, the sentence you got for cannabis is fair?

JAMES: They have to give you something. It's a crime, I committed a crime, there's a law, aye, I broke a law. I've got to be punished for it and the judge probably thought four year seven month for that was right. He's a judge, you ken what I mean, he should know, the right sentence for it.

As James's quote illustrates, for him the fact that he had broken a law meant that punishment was acceptable, but he did not see his imprisonment as just deserts for the harm he had caused. Many others also referred to their infraction of the law as the only necessary explanation of their sentence.

I suppose it is fair enough, aye, I know we don't all agree all the time with the sentences that are dished out, but that's just part and parcel of it, I suppose. Part and parcel, if you commit a crime, you should know now, you are old enough now to know the consequences. (Neil)

No, the sentences have been justifiable. Because I shouldn't have bloody committed the crime in the first place. You know what I mean, there's rules and regulations that you've got to stick by and that is part of the rule. (Jack)

For my interviewees the level of harm caused was a (usually) sufficient but not necessary reason for acceptance of their sentence – even when the harm was not significant (in their eyes), many still accepted their sentence because of their infraction of the law. This might illustrate that they recognised the legitimacy of the courts to uphold the laws of the land, but may also be caused by other factors (discussed below).

A few of the men commented that they felt the court did not understand enough of the context of their lives to be able to judge them. Several interviewees felt that their Social Enquiry Reports did not contain enough depth and that their circumstances were ignored in favour of their criminal record. For example, Chris felt that the court should have realised that, although he was couriering a significant amount of drugs, he was a heroin addict himself and therefore more a victim of his dealer forcing him into couriering to clear a debt than 'a bad person and a drug dealer'. Similarly, Peter became angry during the interview about the lack of insight the jury and judge had into his childhood.

So why should I be judged by people that don't know me, don't know where I come from, where I've been and these people are judging me. They don't know the, the, the upbringing I've had and (.) the things I've just told you, children's care, two year old, foster care, feeling like I've not got family, pushed to the side. (Peter)

He felt, accordingly, that the court did not have the standing to judge him.

Issues with procedural justice were also mentioned in several of the interviews, although these were more often to do with police procedures than with what occurred in the courtroom. Perceptions of police injustice were most often related to drug offences; several of the men thought the police had induced someone to betray them by offering to let this person go free; a procedure they felt was unfair.

I think the guy who gave me the drugs sorta set me up, know what I mean, eh? Cause he got lifted for a driving while disqualified on the previous weekend, then on the Wednesday, I think it was, a Wednesday night, he dropped it [the drugs] off and within five minutes my door was in, know what I mean?... That's what I don't like about the police, why do they do that sort of stuff, know what I mean?... If that is the case then I think it's unfair. (Smitty)

Feelings of injustice in these cases were especially strong when the person cooperating with the police was seen as more culpable, for example because they dealt in higher volumes of drugs, than the interviewee. The most serious failing possible of the criminal justice system was evident in two interviews. Alex and Gordon maintained they had been convicted of crimes they had not committed.

Then I got the charge for this, which sort of struck me a bit, because it was something I never done, but it was something I had to try and fight and had to try and fight through it, you know what I mean? And I ended up losing [laughs uncomfortably]. (Gordon)

Like I said, I mean I/ I still maintain my innocence, you know, and I think in the longer term I will be able to demonstrate the suppression [of evidence] and this will be overturned. (Alex)

Gordon and Alex's accounts provided a crucial insight into how the men framed their sentences. In their cases, especially, I expected vehement opposition, but instead found an overall story of acceptance. They gave reasons why, despite their professed innocence, it was nonetheless acceptable that they had been given a long-term sentence.

> Maybe a sentence was just waiting to happen. Maybe no/ maybe not as much or as long a sentence, but with the crowd I was running about with at the time, pretty much, see, there was maybe a sentence in the making, you know what I mean? (Gordon)

> In a technical sense, it's both a miscarriage of justice and a malicious prosecution, simply, you know? But, that said, eeh (.) I kind of shrug my shoulders with it, because at the end of the day, I was up to a lot of no good. (Alex)

Rather than evaluating their sentence in the light of the crime of which they had been convicted, they assessed it in terms of their whole lives: what they had done in the past or might have done in the future. In this, they were similar to Casper's respondents who were not guilty of the crime for which they had received their sentence: they also felt that their 'general guilt' meant that they deserved punishment (Casper, 1972).

Shades of acceptance

The way in which Alex and Gordon neutralised the injustice of their sentence highlighted the way in which other respondents, with less serious complaints, did the same. As already mentioned, those who thought they had not caused much harm often justified their sentence with reference to their infraction of the law. Furthermore, even though most of the men felt imprisonment failed in its purpose(s), as discussed in the previous chapter, this did not lead to anger that was sustained throughout their accounts. Especially those coming to the end of their sentence seemed to need to accept their sentence and tended to resist questions that might have threatened that acceptance. Therefore, the following sections focus on the views of this group and on the factors that played a role in driving their acceptance just before release, before comparing this with the attitudes of the men on licence.

Besides taking a 'general guilt' approach to the legitimacy of the sentence or justifying it as a consequence of infringement of the law, many of those at the end of their sentence positioned their sentence as a positive event in their lives; whether because it provided an opportunity for change (on which more in Chapter 5), or because it allowed them to avoid fates worse than imprisonment.

I think a small sentence, I'd probably be out, back in again, out, back in again, so I wouldn't be sitting at forty year old, thinking this 'I've had enough', I might still be going in and out, in and out, till fifty or SIXTY even, you ken what I mean. And now I'm forty, I'm not coming back in again, you ken what I mean. So it has been positive. (James)

So in a way, I was better off to come here anyway, because I was/ the way I was going, I was going about/ drink, drugs outside, I would have probably ended up killing myself, you know, so I think this is more or less/ the jail saves a lot of people, it really does, you know. (Graham)

Again, the reasons interviewees gave for their acceptance were instrumental rather than normative. While statements such as the ones by James and Graham above were often expressed in quite tentative language, using words like 'probably', 'in a way', 'kind of' and 'maybe', they described the interviewees' overall attitudes to their sentence more closely than the statements condemning their sentence on the grounds of not following the rules or not being based on shared beliefs. Compare for example Gordon saying 'I think it is a joke' and 'where is the justice system in that?' (p. 63) to his quote starting 'maybe a sentence was just waiting to happen' (p. 68). While the condemnation of his sentence (for an offence he maintained he did not commit) was more confidently expressed and therefore seems to be based on more deeply held beliefs, the phrase that best sums up his attitude to his sentence as expressed throughout his narrative is:

But, like I say, I have gained a lot from being in jail, not that it's anything to be proud of, but (.) qualifications and courses and certificates and I've tried to do everything to benefit me for getting out.

At times in his narrative he goes further, with statements such as:

It makes me, makes me in a good way feel now, looking back, that maybe the best thing was that I have done this sentence.

Interestingly, almost all of the interviewees at the end of their sentence expressed resignation or optimism about the sentence, even those who evaluated it negatively for one or several of the reasons outlined above. Even where stated reasons for seeing the sentence as fair (such as ones of 'general guilt' or having infringed on the law) were quite tentative, they seemed to allow these men to create narratives that did not revolve around opposition.

That not opposing their sentence was important to many of the interviewees was apparent in their discomfort in discussing their sentence in normative terms. As this was the main purpose of the interview, I usually prompted them to do so and would point out inconsistencies in their accounts, which often led them to become defensive of their sentence. Accordingly, I sometimes felt I was overstepping the mark in insisting on questioning the link between crime and punishment. As my notes on my interview with James record:

> I think I was too focused on the fairness questions. It seemed like he really did not want to answer these, he kept avoiding engaging with them, so there was not much point anyway.

From the transcript, his avoidance of normative questions is clear. The following is only a short excerpt of this part of the interview:

MS: I get that, maybe I am asking a question you can't answer, but I'm wondering, why is prison the right thing, four years in prison?

JAMES: Because there's nothing else.

MS: What do you mean?

JAMES: Well, what other thing can we give as a punishment?

MS: I don't know, probation, a fine, nothing, capital punishment.

JAMES: They have to give you something. It's a crime, I committed a crime, there's a law, aye, I broke a law. I've got to be punished for it and the judge probably thought four year seven month for that was right. He's a judge, you ken what I mean, he should know, the right sentence for it.

MS: So you feel it is not up to you to question the connection?

JAMES: If it were up to me, I would have got away with it, you ken what I mean? But it's not up to me.

MS: [Laughs]. Well, if you were sentencing somebody with the same record and the same circumstances, what would you think would be the right sentence?

JAMES: (.) Well, but I'm not a judge, though. My attitude would be different from what I'm thinking now, you ken what I mean? If I was the judge it would probably be the same.

With James, I was especially and overly persistent, because he said he disagreed with the law against dealing cannabis which had led to his conviction, and so his avoidance is especially clear. However, many of the men at the end of their sentence similarly deflected normative questions.

MS: And what sentence would you give to someone who had had the same part/

PETER: /I wouldn't go and sentence no one, I wouldn't put myself in that position, it's not for me to judge people.

The extent to which the men defended, accepted or welcomed their sentence varied. Some merely neutralised their own or possible objections to their sentence, leading to a lack of opposition but no actual endorsement, while others more actively defended their sentence, most likely because they needed it to play a transformative role in their lives (see Chapter 5). However, some level of acceptance or acquiescence in one's sentence was almost universal amongst those who were about to be released. The fact that even those who maintained they were innocent told this type of account begs the question why this is the case, as it seems that they, especially, worked hard to construct an account that allowed them to accept the unacceptable.

Impact of prison environment at the end of the sentence

One of the main factors driving acceptance was the need to negotiate the pains of imprisonment. This section first examines this connection, before placing it in the context of the men's wider adaptation to their confinement and the functions of this adaptation. The next section examines the relationship between acceptance and the prison environment by discussing the two men for whom coping with imprisonment did *not* mean accepting their sentence. I then go on to consider the consequences of the wider adaptation strategy for life after release, by exploring the accounts of the men on licence.

Interviewees clearly and repeatedly indicated that opposing their sentence would have made their confinement more difficult to cope with.

It's still fair, I'm here, I'm doing it. *It doesn't have to be fair, that's how I'm dealing with it.* (Peter, emphasis added)

But, the way I see it is, clearly I would rather not be here, but you don't have a choice. You've got to cope, you've got to just put your head in a place where, you know, you don't feel, eehm, unduly frustrated or anxious or (.) or whatever. (Alex)

You have to say 'this is it, this is me for the next x amount of years, I'm not going out anyway, so (.), you know, just get on with it, try to make the best of it. There's no point in walking about all day with a bucket of depression, because (.) pfff, it doesn't get you anywhere, does it? (Neil)

Narrative research has been criticised for endorsing individual accounts which 'float in a social vacuum' (Atkinson, 1997, p. 339), but in these narratives there were several indications that acceptance of the sentence was not a strategy adopted by individuals in isolation. The quotes above have subtle differences. Peter described his view of the situation in the first person singular and thereby as an individual strategy, but Alex switched to the second person when describing the need to cope, and Neil used the second person throughout. This implies that they think the same pressures are experienced by others in the same situation and suggests that acquiescing with one's sentence is a recognised strategy. This is supported by James's description of observing others' reactions and his recommendation of acceptance as the best way to cope:

> A lot of people that come in say 'oh, I shouldn't have got that, it was too big', I think that makes a sentence harder, because you just accept it, that's what you got, you broke the law and you got caught and that was it. You'll probably get on with your sentence a lot better. (James)

Furthermore, prisoners often used the same phrases to describe their attitude to their sentence, with phrases like 'getting your head down' and 'getting on with it' repeated across interviews. This way of overcoming any feelings of injustice is transferred between prisoners, and a response to the conditions they all faced. It was acceptance induced by the need to cope (or *coping-acceptance*) rather than acceptance because the sentence was normatively just.

Two interviewees *did* tell a (partial) narrative of opposition to their sentence (see below), which shows that this response to imprisonment is not inevitable. For most, though, accepting their sentence made their prison experience less painful. This echoes previous findings in the criminological literature. Sykes (1958) found that the most admired stance in the prison he researched was that of the 'real man', who bears his sentence with equanimity. Similarly, Crewe (2009) found that prisoners who managed their own problems without complaining often accrued respect, while those who could not handle their sentence were disparaged. However, while these authors describe an admired stoicism that involves being uncomplaining about hardship, in this research the lack of opposition was described as actually *reducing* the hardships of imprisonment, rather than as a product of brave forbearance.

Accepting the sentence was not an isolated adjustment, but was described as part of a wider adaptation process, which diminished the pains of imprisonment more generally. Phrases such as 'getting your head down'[1] were not only used in relation to accepting one's sentence, but also had a wider meaning of forgetting about anything not immediately relevant to prison life. This included the amount of time left on one's sentence.

> See, when you've got years to go and you just don't think about it and it's just (.) your head's in here, this is your life in here you know what I mean, in this wee small surrounding. (Doug)

Shutting out thoughts of loved ones outside was part of this process, with several prisoners going so far as to limit phone contact and visits in order to make their sentence easier to bear.

> You can't get on thinking about [his daughter], then you're going to start thinking about, what is she up to out there, who's she with, you know what I mean, you can't just/ you can't think about it. You have to try and put it in the back of your head for a wee bit, y'know? Bad enough even going/ taking your visits, it's still putting your head on the fence, you don't wanna go over the fence. (Graham)

As Graham pointed out, thinking about your family means thinking about the world outside prison, which is painful. Ian and many others also commented on how closer relationships made for more painful imprisonment.

> That's what I'm saying. Because I've got a wean now, this has been the hardest sentence I've done. This sentence has broke my back, you could say, you know what I'm talking about, because all I've done is think about my son.

Others gave examples that illustrated how not 'keeping your head inside the walls', or maintaining circumscribed horizons, contributed to the pains of imprisonment.

> You're in tears most nights just wondering what/ when it comes to the weekend you're wondering what's going on outside, you know what your girlfriend's up to, if they're all having a laugh, having a party, do you know, you could be there, you're missing out on your

(.) my wee cousin, she had her wee girl, you know I missed all that, I missed so much. (Mohammed)

Separation was difficult for the men I spoke to because they missed their loved ones, which then emphasised their incarceration and made it difficult to forget the outside, but also because their incarceration made relationships problematic. First of all, contacting family members could be difficult, which led to frustration and worries:

I would say sort of a lot of the bad moments, for me anyway, person-ally, is when I am trying to phone my son and every time you phone him, he has, obviously, a mobile phone and it goes on to the answering machines, but when they are on answering machines it is still taking your money away. So you see the wee digits going, you are phoning your son, you've only got (five or six quid) on the phone, you see your money going like that, psssht. (Neil)

Brain damage, you know what I'm talking about? I used to phone her all the time and (.) the phone would ring, she wouldn't answer it or the phone would be off and then you're pure raging. Eehm, I had a mobile phone at the time and it was just non-stop phoning. And it was just, it done your head in, you know what I'm talking about, you knew the phone was going to ring, but you still phone it. (Ian)

These quotes emphasise the powerlessness of the incarcerated; it is not within their control to maintain contact, only to cut it off. If people do not answer the phone, reply to letters or visit, there is nothing prisoners can do. Furthermore, the repetitiveness of life inside meant that contact that did take place often became superficial and strained.

My friends and that will 'aye book us a visit' an stuff like that and I'm like that 'nah, I'll not', 'cause I don't really like visits because, see when you're in here, that hour in the visiting room it's a long time, there's a lot of uncomfortable pauses of silence because you've not got much to talk about 'cause it's like ground hog day in here. Every day during the week is the same and every weekend is the same, see you've not really got much to talk about at a visit, know what I mean, you end up big uncomfortable pauses of silence. (Doug)

Cutting off contact in this situation solves several problems: it reduces thoughts of those outside, thereby minimising the pain of missing them, it helps to maintain control over relationships and means that they are not diminished through superficial interactions. Far from all of the interviewees at the end of their sentence chose to limit interactions with their loved ones, but it was a common coping strategy. This is worrying, given the research evidence that maintaining contact with those outside (and especially family) helps to maintain identity roles and to reduce reoffending upon release (for example Bosworth, 1996; Cullen, 1994; Forste, Clarke and Bahr, 2011; Mills and Codd, 2008; Social Exclusion Unit, 2002).

Maintaining circumscribed horizons had two dimensions and, accordingly, two functions. Limiting their horizons in space to fit the confines of the prison walls allowed the men to ignore what they had lost for long periods at a time.

> Because I'm in the jail, I just forget about the outside world. It helps me to get on with it in here, you ken what I mean. Because if I don't have an outside, I can't bring it in. This is my world just now, you ken what I mean, I just deal with this. (James)

By living their life as if there were no outside to miss, the men reduced the pain inherent in their imprisonment. Limiting one's temporal horizons was, according to interviewees, the best way to speed up time. Not looking forward to anything, but being busy and getting immersed in the prison routine meant that the days passed more easily.

> I can remember when it was June, I can remember saying to people, I was like that 'that's six months by already, it doesn't seem like two days ago it was Christmas' you know what I mean, that part flew in. See August/September, because there was a lot of rigmarole about me going to the Castle and stuff like that, the time sort of slowed down. (Doug)

Prison conditions, then, seemed to be at least one driving factor in the lack of opposition found amongst the prisoners. Opposing one's sentence, like thinking of family and friends outside, would puncture the circumscribed horizons maintained by the men, and thereby make their sentence more difficult to bear.

There are similarities between the acquiescence described here and the notion of 'dull compulsion' (Carrabine, 2004; Sparks et al., 1996): the way in which prison routines make the (unjust) power relations in a prison seem inevitable and therefore not worth opposing to prisoners. While this concept was developed in the study of power relations internal to the prison, it also has a role to play in the men's acquiescence in their sentence.

> Just a sort of sense of (.) of frustration, wasted opportunity or contained or repressed energy or ambition or enthusiasm, you know, all that sort of has to be kind of reigned in, you know, whilst you're here. You know, you've got to sort of make, well I find, that, you know, you've got to make a conscious effort to kind of (.) personally speaking, you know, like a bear going into hibernation. You've got to make a conscious effort to slow down your impulses, because otherwise you'd drive yourself mad, you know, like a caged tiger. I mean, you've got to, you've got to recognise that you can do nothing about the containment, so you have to adapt to it. You know, you have to get your mind in the right place for (.) just, just (.) getting on with that, you know? (Alex)

While Alex's quote suggests that the reality of imprisonment is indeed 'dulling' and that, in order to adapt to it he did have to let go of feelings of unfairness, it is not clear that it was the routines of imprisonment, rather than just its inevitability, that led to his acquiescence. The sentence imposed is even more inevitable than the existing power relations in prison: while demands may be made about prison conditions or greater respect from staff, collectively opposing individual sentences is impossible. Tellingly, almost all those at the end of their prison term accepted their sentence, but there were many instances where they described opposing the regime or decisions made by staff, demonstrating that there was more space for opposition in this regard.

> I refused to go into a double cell when I got back from the courts. I told them to put me down in the punishment block, and they're single cells there. They were trying to get me doubled up, I said no, it's not going to happen, just put me down the digger. (Dan)

In contrast, in relation to the sentence the only recourse is the appeals process, but once this is completed, there are no further opportunities for opposition that may lead to a different outcome (with the possible exception of escape). This may be why the interviewees focused more on the inevitability of their imprisonment than on its routines. For them, the dull compulsion was a product of 'the sense that there are no alternatives and that one's subordination is inevitable and unalterable' (Crewe, 2009, p. 83), leading to what Sparks et al. call the 'the-put-up-with-as-inevitable' (1996, p. 85). In addition, for the interviewees the inevitability of imprisonment was not the only driving factor for acceptance: instrumental benefits (see also Crewe 2009) and, more compellingly, a need for a positive narrative (see Chapter 5) also played an important role.

However, the concept of 'dull compulsion' and the impact of routine on acceptance can also illuminate how sentences of imprisonment can become routine. For several of the men at the end of their sentence and on licence, imprisonment had become such a normal feature of their life that they no longer questioned it in any way, and saw it more as respite than as a punishment. Their accounts have already been discussed briefly with regards to these men denying the deterrent function of prison in Chapter 3. Here, their accounts show how accepting one's sentence, even a long-term prison sentence, can be a form of acceptance 'based upon habit or routine', which Bottoms characterises as most likely to occur without reflection (Bottoms, 2001). This was the case for Ian, Jack and Tony, with elements of this kind of *routine acceptance* also present in the accounts of others. These were men who were ambivalent about leaving prison, had found doing so difficult and described prison as the most comfortable place for them to be.

> It's getting to the stage that, if I find out on the fourteenth I've not got a house for going out, I'm thinking about refusing to lib myself, you know what I'm talking about. (Ian)
>
> Just, I enjoyed it and I didn't want to come out, you should have saw the state of me when I came out, really bad, aye. (Tony)
>
> As I said to you earlier, it didn't bother me one bit, you know what I mean, going in or whatever, cause it was like a second home to me. (Jack)

Just as offending can become a routine that no longer involves a decision to offend (Tunnell, 1992), so imprisonment can become a routine that no longer needs an explanation or justification, and becomes 'taken-for-granted' (Sparks et al., 1996, p. 89). These men, accordingly, did not reflect on the (in)justice of their sentence of their own accord. For them, it was not so much the impact of the prison environment that prevented opposition, but the routine of frequent and repeated imprisonment.

Exceptions

While the pressure of having to cope with a long-term prison sentence was there for all those interviewed at the end of their sentence, the above should not give the impression that all these men coped in the same way. As Jewkes (2005) has noted in relation to life-sentenced prisoners, while the structures of imprisonment influence prisoners, they do not determine their actions and perceptions. Not everyone had accepted their sentence, with injustice a major theme in two of the interviews. Devan was young, 20, when he was imprisoned for his first ever offence. He, like Jewkes' (2005) life sentence prisoners, appealed to a non-offender identity, remembering his past positive identities of the good son and brother, school leaver with good prospects and exceptional employee. The description of these identities took up long stretches of the interview. He was imprisoned for seven and a half years for what he maintained were trumped up drug charges. While generally accepting of the criminal justice system, and even his imprisonment, he strongly felt his sentence should have been shorter.

> I'm not saying that I shouldn't be in here, for the crime that I committed, because obviously I committed a crime, but it's about the sentencing that I got for the crime. There's guys in here that's committed murder and got lesser time than me…so (.) why give out the kind of punishment that they give out, how can they justify that within themselves, or do they even care when they give out sentences like that, do they just think: 'ah, okay, he's committed an offence' at the back of her head or his head, he is probably thinking 'I already know what I'm going to give this guy, it doesn't make a difference what he says or what he does, he is still going to get that sentence.' And that's what they do, isn't it? (Devan)

Devan was also the only interviewee who revealed any hostility towards the judge who sentenced him.

Peter at first told a very positive account of his imprisonment, saying that he had been given the sentence he deserved and that this term of imprisonment had changed him, so that he would not offend again in the future (for a fuller account of such narratives see Chapter 5).

> I think I'm a good person now, it take me to come to prison and (.) hurt, well, be involved in a murder and sell drugs in the streets to realise that, lots of things I shouldn't be doing…It's probably been/ it's been a wake-up call for me, I tell you that, so I'm glad I got this sentence.…Because I needed to come here and fucking change. (.) To learn, you ken what I mean? Not to be like that. To/ my values and all, my family. I want my family to see I've changed. (Peter)

Here Peter seemed to fit into the category of prisoners described by Crewe (2009) as 'enthusiasts': he condemned his past actions and embraced prison as an opportunity to change. However, at a certain point in the interview his perspective changed to one in which he was victimised by the system and in which he would have matured in any case, and would have been better off outside prison where he would have been able to make more positive changes in his life. He moved to a version of events where his background in care, for which he held the system responsible, had played a large part in his offending. He thought more should be done to help looked after children and that the system was failing in this regard. While he felt that, in his own case, more information should have been made available to the court, he also said that he was institutionalised and saw the prison as his home. He could not see an alternative to his imprisonment and thereby, while he condemned the system, he accepted his sentence.

> I don't know how, how, (.) what the fuck they could do, ken what I mean. Maybe say, 'look this kid has fucking just put his hands up to what he's done, he knows he's done something wrong', but I'll keep on doing things wrong anyway, ken what I mean, so it's not, that's why I just agree with it. I'm, I'm going to get into trouble again, I probably will get into trouble again, even though I don't want to, I'll probably end up back in prison, so (.) ten years is probably good for me. (Peter)

For both these interviewees, this was their first long-term prison sentence. It is interesting that while for Devan prison could be seen as an interruption of his life course, for Peter, who felt institutionalised and at home in the prison, this was not the case. For Peter telling a story of victimisation seems to have, at one point in the interview, become preferable to a narrative of personal transformation. Why this shift occurred is not entirely clear from the transcript and recording, but his position seemed to change after he acknowledged that he had also felt transformed after previous (short-term) sentences, but returned to offending.

> MS: But when you say you kind of had that same outlook after your shorter sentences.
> PETER: Aye
> MS: Do you feel different now from then?
> PETER: No, that's the thing. I, I, I'll/ foolish, that's what I'm saying, I'll probably end up doing the things I was doing before. Because

> I won't be able to get a job, I've tried to get a job, many a times.
> Every time I've been released from prison I went to the job centre,
> and I tried getting jobs, and it's just not there for me.

Here he might have felt the more positive narrative became untenable,
which caused him to shift to a narrative that allowed him to express
some of his anger at the system, which was noticeable during the
remainder of the interview.

Impact of prison environment and legitimacy on licence

While most of the men who were coming to the end of their sentence
spoke of their strategy of circumscribing their horizons with something
akin to pride in their ability to cope with the prison environment, the same
strategy played a very different role in the accounts of the men on licence,
who frequently described how adapting to the prison environment had
left them institutionalised. Limiting their horizons in prison meant that
they now had a difficult time coping with the complexities and demands
of life outside. One source of difficulty was resuming normal relationships,
which seemed at least in part to be a consequence of the withdrawal from
loved ones described by those at the end of their sentence.

> TIM: But sometimes I miss some elements of prison where I can (.)
> shut my door and escape for a wee while, I enjoyed that (.) with
> the (.). The troubles will go away when you shut the door.
> MS: So why can you do that in prison and not at home for example?
> TIM: Because you've got family and you've got people depending on
> you and you've got to face people and you can't bottle everything
> up and shut it all away, you've got to, got to go out there and face
> everybody so.

Tim found it hard to get used to the normal demands of relationships
again: to have people depend on him and to share his thoughts and feelings with them in turn. Others described a similar tendency to avoid the
company of others after having adapted to the isolation of prison.

> I don't like leaving the house and I'm quite happy in my own company.
> I mean I don't crave attention or anything like that and/ my cousin
> was phoning me the other day as well and asking me to go for a drink
> and I hope he wasn't offended, but I was like that 'I can't be bothered
> with company the now'. And that's just typical of me now. (Lino)

Lino contrasted this new introversion to his previous approach to life, when he 'used to enjoy being in the middle of everything'. It is worth noting that Lino had only been on licence for seven months, but Tim had been released more than five years previously. This illustrates that problems with relationships do not necessarily reduce over time. Tim explicitly commented that adapting to life outside was more difficult for him than adapting to imprisonment, saying 'and it's (.) adjusting that way is probably harder, it's harder outside now than it was in prison'.

Other difficulties encountered by those on licence as a result of their adaptation to the prison regime included needing routines, difficulties with taking responsibility for their own decisions and providing for themselves (see also Burnett and Maruna, 2006).

> You've got/ you get your three meals a day, you don't need to cook them, they're cooked for you, you get them. You get woken up in the morning by the officers, your own alarm clock basically so they're coming in and wakening you up. You've got your shower across from your cell, you go and get your shower, you get organ-ised for work in the morning, it doesn't matter what kind of crim-inal record you've got, you've always got a job in prison ... and it's SO easy, it's unbelievable, you come back from work, brilliant go for a shower, put the PlayStation on, feet up and that's you for the night. (Mohammed)

Mohammed, who at other points in his interview commented on how difficult prison had been for him, contrasted the above with his current situation, where he had very little money but many bills, and employ-ment was a remote prospect while those around him worked. Jack simi-larly realised that, after his imprisonment, he found it difficult to react appropriately to everyday stressors.

> JACK: I get worked up over nothing, over NOTHING and I get all stressed over it.
> MS: And is that because of being in prison for so long do you think or is that just you?
> JACK: It must be something like that, because I get really, really stressed out and it's over nothing. I'm talking about I get all hyped up and want to crack up. (Jack)

Some of the men on licence were trying to recreate tight routines in their lives outside, in order to make coping easier.

But I like to run, you know I like to have my daily routine so I know what I'm doing each day, that's prison isn't it? I think that's how I liked prison, because I knew I was getting up first thing in the morning, go down to the treadmill and run for an hour and a half and, you know, do things like that. (Tony)

This imposition of a routine on oneself has been found to be important post-release in avoiding reoffending (Hartwell, McMakin, Tansi and Bartlett, 2010). On the other hand, Hockey (2012), himself a one-time prisoner, sees the post-prison need for routines as potentially criminogenic. He writes of his experiences upon release:

Although the enclosed routine imposed by the system had gone and the internalised routine of time markers had become redundant, the processing style had remained. Whilst it lacked the structure of imprisonment, it was still dysfunctional in relying on the concrete thinking of basic routines and *in the absence of something more constructive*, old habits and familiarity soon returned to fill that void. (Hockey, 2012, p. 73, emphasis added)

The 'absence of something more constructive' experienced by many of the men on licence was a source of great frustration. Many of them were trying to get jobs, but failing because of their criminal record (see Chapter 5).

The descriptions of the difficulties the men on licence faced due to their experience of imprisonment more closely match the concept of institutionalisation than the one of prisonisation. While the two are not completely distinct, prisonisation is a term coined by Clemmer (1958, cited in Wheeler, 1961, p. 697) who used it to refer to the impact of the inmate code on individual prisoners. By accepting the prisoner culture, one of antisocial values opposing the norms of prison staff and society at large, the prisoner has difficulty in adapting to life outside once he is released. Wheeler (1961) qualified this, by finding that the adherence to the inmate code diminished as prisoners approached their release date. However, the men I interviewed very rarely described having had their values changed through interactions with other prisoners, although occasionally this had made them *more* pro-social, as described in Chapter 3. This may well be because the way in which power now operates in the prison prevents an oppositional inmate code from forming. As Crewe has noted, 'the strength of a subculture depends upon common plight, mutual resistance, relative isolation and a lack of mobility out of the shared predicament' (2009, p. 245), conditions that were not present in the prison he studied and are likely to also be absent in other modern UK prisons, including the prisons in which the interviewees served time.

The concept of institutionalisation has received attention in Goffman's book *Asylums* (1968), an examination of different 'total institutions', ones in which people live round the clock, including psychiatric hospitals, boarding schools, monasteries and prisons. In such institutions, those who live there undergo 'role dispossession', in that they have only the role of inmate to fulfil rather than the variety of roles they had before they were admitted. They have no say in the way they live their lives, which is therefore also no longer their responsibility. Instead they are managed through strict routines:

> minute segments of a person's line of activity may be subject to regulations and judgements by staff...rob[bing] the individual of an opportunity to balance his needs and objectives in a personally efficient way. (Goffman, 1968, p. 43)

This loss of responsibility and being cut off from meaningful relationships and roles in which they were relied upon found expression in the interviewees' accounts. In talking about the difficulties these prison conditions created for their adaptation to life outside, it was striking how often those on licence actually used the word 'institutionalisation' (seven out of nine did so at least once in their interview), compared to those still in prison (amongst whom Peter was the only one to use it).

> So, eehm, it's been very hard, because I think I've been institutionalised. (Lino)
>
> because I've been in and out, in and out, in and out, it's just like a second home to me, do you know what I'm meaning. (.) They maybe call it institutionalised if you want, that's probably the word for it. (Jack)
>
> I don't know you (.) the term institutionalised just says it all, you just / it's like learning anything you just (.) roll with the punches but (.) it gets easier. (Tim)
>
> Well, I think I'm institutionalised, because (.) my wife points out a lot of things to me. (Stephen)
>
> a lot of people I talk to say I'm institutionalised, eh (.) and in there you've no worries, you don't need to worry about a wife or a partner. (Tony)

Equally striking is the way in which many used the term as a concept external to themselves: one that had been applied by others ('they maybe call it', 'a lot of people I talk to say') or framed it as a word they would not usually use ('that's probably the word for it', 'the term…says it all'). It may be that this word was introduced into their vocabulary by their social worker or other professionals. More pertinent to the current analysis, however, is the way they distanced themselves from the coping techniques used by the men at the end of their sentence, which presumably should allow them to see their sentence without the constraints upon those who were still imprisoned.

When analysing their views of their sentence, however, it becomes clear that this is only partly true. Amongst the men on licence, there was still very little sense of anger or opposition about their sentence, but comparing their acceptance to that of the men at the end of their sentence is not straightforward. While the latter group included two men who maintained they were innocent, which meant opposition was to be expected from them, amongst the men on licence there were no such cases. It is therefore easier to see this group's acquiescence as genuine agreement with their sentence. In some cases, this accurately captures their accounts: Andy and Mark both felt their sentence was deserved for the harm they inflicted on others and Smitty felt his sentence was very lenient. Tim's case perhaps came closest to those of Alex and Gordon. He was sentenced by a judge uncertain of his culpability, after having stabbed a friend in a fight. He, like those at the end of their sentence, did refer to the impact of the prison environment in shaping his attitude towards his sentence.

> It's a case of maturing and learning to take, take things as they are and (.). As I say, but if you keep dwelling on it and you're going down the bad path and trying to fight it, it'll keep you there. (Tim)

Tim, too, came to *coping-acceptance*, rather than acceptance based on normative reasons. There were other instances, too, where those on licence seemed, like the men at the end of their sentence, to need to accept their sentence and used similar techniques to do so. For example, Mohammed referred to his 'general guilt' right after asserting prison had not been helpful.

> I don't think prison did me any good anyway. Eehm, to be honest I mean maybe it was/ but I think it probably was the right thing to do because the way my temper was, I would probably have committed another offence anyway, quite (.) soon after that if I'd have stayed out anyway. (Mohammed)

Contradictions were also still a frequent feature of accounts in which reasons were given to think the sentence unjust. For example Lino accepted an earlier sentence of ten years wholeheartedly, because of the serious consequences his crime could have had, but was much more ambivalent about his most recent sentence. At first he said that, even though it had been a victimless crime, he deserved his punishment.

> It is still no excuse for carrying a knife either, and quite rightly so that I got the four year, because I had been caught with a knife before when I was younger, so it wasn't my first offence for that.

However, later in his interview, while still 'understanding' his sentence, he no longer approved of it.

> I think/ I certainly think with regards to four years for carrying an offensive weapon, (.) I understand why they're thinking that way and they're trying to be as eehm, as strict as possible, but I would only consider/ if I was the judge I would only consider giving somebody a four year sentence for carrying a knife if that knife was used in any kind of violence.....I think, I think they're trying to hang me every-thing together, they're trying to tar everybody with the same brush, which I don't think, I don't think that's the way forward, *I certainly don't think that's a fair system*. (.) Regards to (.) to me, I suppose I did know the consequences. (emphasis added)

Finally, he roundly decried his sentence as having been unfair and ineffective:

> The four year sentence it was just/ it felt to me like it was a complete waste a' two year, eight month of my life, a complete waste (.) for what?

The similarities between the accounts of the men on licence and those still in prison suggest that the former had not re-evaluated their sentence upon release of their own accord. Lino's quotes, however, also highlight a subtle difference between the accounts of some of the men on licence and those still in prison. Whereas the latter often used their infraction of the law as a way to justify their sentence and resisted normative thinking about their offence, Lino did the opposite. He acknowledged that he knew the possible consequences of carrying a knife, but did not accept that this meant he should have been given a long-term prison sentence. He was also willing to put himself in the judge's shoes and to consider what would have been more just in this situation. Other licensees, too, seemed less defensive of their sentence and more open to questions around its legitimacy in the interview. Neither were they as invested in their sentence as a trigger of personal change (see the next chapter). Earlier in this chapter I have described how reluctant James and others at the end of their sentence were to consider normative questions. Those on licence, like Lino above, were more willing to consider the right punishment for their crime, sometimes spontaneously putting themselves in the position of the judge who sentenced them, and were less staunch in their justification of their sentence.

> Like I've said, I would have maybe/ I don't know, if I was the judge I might have sentenced me to a bit longer actually, to be honest, because the guy was stabbed like 13 times or something do you know what I mean, in his heart and all that nearly. (Andy)

> MS: So do you think your sentences have been fair, have they been just?
> MOHAMMED: To be honest, they were fair, aye.
> MS: Yeah and do you think sending people to prison is kind of the right response to the thing you did?
> MOHAMMED: No, I don't, no. Because prison's (.) it's not helped me, it's made me (.) I am actually (.) you'll may not think, I'm actually (.) [silent laugh] see I'm scared to go to a job interview.

Furthermore, those on licence referred less often to the constraints put on their thinking about their sentence by the prison environment (for an exception, see Tim's earlier quote on p. 84). Instead they frequently described a different trajectory in attitude: one where they had been angry with their sentence to begin with, but had come to accept it because of greater maturity or understanding, rather than because this was the only way to cope with the prison experience. Tim's earlier quote combines both these elements. Mohammed attributed his change of heart to a course offered by the prison:

> MS: And you said that with this last sentence you felt that it was unfair, initially. That it was their fault?
> MOHAMMED: Yeah, at first, but as time went on you kinda (.) once I done anger management actually.

This emphasis on maturity or learning might be a preferable way to explain acceptance of the sentence once the term of imprisonment is over and the need to survive the prison sentence is no longer present. Seeing yourself as having grown, rather than as having been constrained, provides a more positive narrative in that it ascribes a more active role to the self and is more likely to have significance beyond release.

As with the men at the end of their sentence, there was an exception to the general acceptance amongst those on licence. Stephen told a narrative in which opposition to his sentence and to his licence supervision were a major theme. As illustrated by his quote on page 65, he felt that the time he had spent in prison on a life sentence had been far too long. When he committed another offence after seven years in the community, he spent another five years in prison, which he also felt had been unfair.

> The second one, the judge in court sentenced me to 33 months, so I think that's what I should have done, 33 months. I don't think the parole board should have held me in any longer. Because the judge deemed the 33 month fitted the crime, because he postponed the court for half an hour and went and he looked up and came back and sentenced me.

Stephen was also the only man on licence I spoke to who was dissatisfied with his social worker and felt under surveillance from social work.

> He's (.) I come in and try and talk to him, even the way I'm talking to you just now. Try and explain a problem to him. He just butts in, shuts me up, shoves me out the door and makes another appointment for next week. That's no good to me, I need somebody I can talk to, and that's where my drug counsellor comes in. But I have to be very, very careful what I say to him, because he's duty bound to pass on information [to social work].

Because people are not good at remembering their own attitudes over long periods of time (Ruspini, 2000) and change the way they see the past in order to make sense of the present (Josselson, 1995) it is not possible to say whether Stephen had always felt this way about his involvement with the criminal justice system, including when he was imprisoned, or whether he re-evaluated his sentence upon release. However, Stephen himself said the following about his attitude while he was in prison:

> You can't get angry then, because if they see the anger I'd have done 29 years. You can't let them see anger because then you haven't learned anything, you're just back to your old ways.

In his retrospective account, at least, Stephen's sense of injustice about his sentence had developed when he had been in prison for the length of time he would have thought fair (15 years), but had to be hidden at the time.

In summary, there were some indications that, with greater distance from the experience of imprisonment, the men on licence were more able to consider their sentence in a normative light. However, they had not done so spontaneously and seemed to only reflect on the fairness of their sentence because they were asked to do so in the interview. While the prison environment's impact on the men's moral reflections might have become less pronounced, it had a lasting and negative impact on their ability to adjust to life after release.

Conclusion

This chapter has discussed how the impact of the prison environment led to acceptance of their sentence for almost all the men I interviewed. But does this acceptance matter? In order to answer that question, it is necessary to ask three further ones. First of all, is the acceptance in the men's accounts likely to have been genuine, or an attempt to avoid negative consequences? Secondly, what does their acceptance of their sentence mean in terms of their sentences' legitimacy? And finally, is the stance taken towards the sentence likely to influence future behaviour?

To answer the first question, it is important to briefly describe the way in which the men were recruited as participants for this research. The initial plan for prisoners coming towards the end of their sentence had been that every prisoner in the research prison who fitted the criteria and had an ICM meeting over the research period would be presented with an information sheet describing the research. They could then indicate whether or not they were interested in taking part. In practice, though, it soon became apparent that the actual recruitment method was much more ad hoc, with the contact staff for the research approaching prisoners who they felt met the criteria. A discussion with one of these staff members was recorded in my research notes as follows:

> 3/12/2009 Recruitment strategy: he looks around the flats to see who is coming out (at flat boards and case conferences). He usually knows

them and speaks to the Hall staff. Does not give me prisoners who have nothing to say. (He knocked on the wood of the table to show they are thick?).

This raises the possibility that only the most compliant of prisoners, with the most positive views of the prison regime, were recruited – leading to higher levels of acceptance of the sentence and regime than would otherwise have been the case. Furthermore, Crewe (2009) argues that statements of support for unjust institutions, or in this case, support for sentences that otherwise appear unjust, are unlikely to be a product of the greater psychological expediency of 'embrac[ing] one's powerlessness [compared] to torment[ing] oneself with the daily recognition of one's subjection' (p. 94). He claims that it is more likely that people publicly agree with rules and regimes which they privately feel are unjust, in order to avoid (further) punishment. If he is correct, then the men might have privately opposed their sentence, but told me that they accepted it, in order to avoid any negative repercussions. I am not in a position to completely refute either one of these possibilities. However, there were indications that these men were neither especially careful in the interview, nor the most compliant of prisoners. First of all, many disclosed actions that merited further punishment during the interview. For example, one of the men admitted to being guilty of several past crimes for which he had been prosecuted but not convicted. He also alluded to other crimes, which had not been detected.

> When, when I was eighteen/ I started committing serious crimes when I was about 19, you know, I'm talking about robberies here, you know, like (.) robbing places, I have to be careful what I'm saying [laughs].

He obviously was aware of the interview context and that what he said *could* be used against him, but seemed to trust the confidentiality of the setting enough to nevertheless disclose such sensitive information. While this was an extreme example, others admitted importing or dealing drugs within the prison, engaging in other forms of illicit trade and undetected past offending. Secondly, the men I spoke to felt free to express anger at the lack of reform and rehabilitation in the prison, as discussed in Chapter **3**. Finally, by their own accounts they were not especially compliant prisoners. For example, Peter described recent interactions with staff in which he was clearly defiant.

I was rolling around with staff across there as well, it was over a hair cut, though. And the prison officer was a pure prick. But he ended up coming across here, once I got out of the digger and that, because he was/ I think he was a bit paranoid, if I bumped into him I was actually going to do something to him.

These examples do not mean that all interviewees felt equally confident about the lack of repercussions of what they said within the interview and many did not share any incriminating information. Neither are Crewe's view and my analysis of the men as largely accepting their sentence mutually exclusive. The number of contradictory views on the fairness of sentences reported here supports a reading of many of the men as being resigned to their sentence rather than thinking it fair, even though they did often position their sentence as fair at least at one point in their accounts. For others, though, exactly the 'psychological expediency of embracing one's powerlessness' Crewe rejects seems to have been a real driver in their acceptance. Furthermore, as I will discuss in the next chapter, for some of the men the fairness of their sentence was so important that their stance went far beyond resignation. They embraced their sentence for the transformative role they envisaged it playing in their lives and can therefore not be characterised as merely acting as if they accepted sentences they privately thought were unfair.

As for the question whether the men's acceptance of their sentences actually renders these legitimate, this depends on one's understanding of legitimacy. As noted in Chapter 2, the most referenced framework of legitimacy in corrections was developed by Tyler and colleagues (Casper et al., 1988; Franke et al., 2010; Jackson et al., 2010; Sunshine and Tyler, 2003) and centres around members of the public accepting that the authorities are entitled to make the decisions they make, and that these should be deferred to. Amongst the interviewees, there did seem to be widespread belief that the criminal justice actors involved in their case were entitled to make the decisions they had made, and to impose the punishment they had imposed, at least amongst those who were coming to the end of their sentence. However, Tyler's conception of legitimacy leaves the *reasons* or basis for these beliefs unexamined.[2] Carrabine's (2004) and Sparks et al.'s (1996) analysis of the impact of 'dull compulsion' on prisoners' attitudes makes it clear that there is a distinction between resignation due to external constraints and acceptance based on a sense of fairness. Rather than truly seen as fair, the sentence might be 'taken for granted' (Sparks et al., 1996, p. 89), just as order can be maintained in the face of illegitimacy, through the 'dull compulsion of prison rituals' (Carrabine, 2004, p. 62). A more useful theory of legitimacy in this context, and one used by Sparks et al. (1996) and Liebling (2004) to examine the legitimacy of prison regimes, is the one formulated by David Beetham (1991), who wrote that mere consent is not enough to make a power relation legitimate unless 'it can be *justified in terms* of [people's] beliefs' (1991, p. 11). He proposes that three conditions need to be fulfilled to achieve legitimacy: one of these is the 'expressed consent' of those subject to the power relation, but he also insists on 'conformity to rules' and 'the justifiability of rules in terms of shared beliefs' (1991, p. 20). When we examine each of the latter conditions in turn, it becomes clear that, while they figured in the men's accounts, and perhaps should have led to perceptions of *illegitimacy,* in fact they were often neutralised. In relation to punishment conforming to the rules, the state's power to punish is based, in the first instance, on the criminal law – only those who have acted against the law can be legitimately punished. As discussed above, the two men who maintained they were innocent of the crime for which they were convicted did negatively evaluate their sentence on this failing, but based their wider narrative on a sense of 'general guilt' and thereby managed to still accept their sentence. Seeing one's sentence in this light is in direct opposition to another principle of law, namely that one is punished in proportion to the index offence(s), not for future or past (undetected) offending. So in effect, the men negated one rule to accept the infringement of another. Other standards the men felt the criminal justice system should abide by were those of consistency, proportionality and having enough knowledge of their circumstances to judge. All three of these standards are reflected in the aims of sentencing in Scotland,[3] but none of the men condemned their sentence because the criminal justice system had not adhered to them. In relation to shared beliefs, the power to punish is based on the criminal law, and therefore for that power to be legitimate the law itself needs to be based on shared beliefs. But the men at the end of their sentence who did not believe that the law they had offended against was right, such as James, still accepted their sentence, on the basis that they had broken the law. This might be an instance of accepting the power to punish because the authority administering that punishment is seen as legitimate; most of the men were uncritical about the criminal justice system as a whole. However, the way in which the men's accounts were constructed, and especially their unwillingness to reflect on normative questions, suggested that their acceptance was due at least in part to the demands of their environment (and the narrative pressures discussed in the next chapter). Their insistence that their punishment was right because they had infringed the law might, then, have been another way of neutralising views that might otherwise lead to feelings of illegitimacy. Beetham's conception of legitimacy also highlights that, although the men at the end of their sentence accepted their sentence, this did not constitute the kind of consent necessary for legitimacy to be bestowed. He employs a very active concept of consent, where it is not the stated agreement of the subordinates in a power relation that matters, but that their actions demonstrate such agreement. Applying this analysis to people's reaction to their sentence alerts us to the fact that there is very little chance to oppose imprisonment or, indeed, to demonstrate one's consent. At the time the sentence is passed, the coercive apparatus leaves the prisoner-to-be with no choice but to be placed within the prison. Once there, he may display anything from 'non-cooperation and passive resistance to open disobedience and militant opposition' (Beetham, 1991, p. 19), all indicators of non-consent according to Beetham, but by then it is difficult to identify whether he is denying the legitimacy of the sentence, or that of the prison regime, or both. While the men's acquiescence may not have been wholly due to 'dull compulsion' or been undercut by a sense of anger (see the next chapter), for many it nevertheless fell short of the type of consent that can legitimise punishment.

Finally, there is the question whether those who accepted their sentence will be more likely to refrain from offending in the future. Sparks and Bottoms have noted that 'only legitimate social arrangements generate normative commitments towards compliance' (1995, p. 48). At least in the case of Gordon and Alex, the two men who said they had been wrongfully convicted, it is difficult not to suspect that, even though they defended their sentence, it is likely that their feelings of allegiance to the criminal justice system and the law will have been diminished rather than increased because of their recent experiences. Bottoms' (2001) analysis of different types of compliance with community penalties can further illuminate the impact of the men's views of their sentence on their future behaviour. He identified four types of compliance: normative compliance (driven by moral considerations, or the attachment to a person), prudential compliance (driven by perceived benefits to complying and costs to non-compliance), constraint-based compliance (which happens when there is no choice but to comply because of structural or physical constraints) and compliance based on habit or routine (p. 90). As noted by Bottoms and above, not complying with a prison sentence is nigh on impossible because imprisonment ensures compliance through imposed physical constraints. However, it is possible to substitute 'acceptance' for 'compliance' for the purposes of this discussion, because the drivers Bottoms identifies in relation to compliance can drive acceptance as well. When applied in this manner, Bottoms' typology illuminates that although many of the men constructed accounts which allowed them to position their sentence as fair (for example by referring to their general guilt, thus presenting themselves as accepting their sentence for normative reasons, akin to Bottoms' 'normative compliance'), in fact their acceptance was often affected by the other three drivers. Normative evaluation of the sentence only seemed to happen in a positive direction, for example where the level of harm was seen as justifying the sentence. However, where there was no agreement between the men's moral judgements (about what should be illegal, or who should have the standing to judge them) and their sentence, or where they said they had been the victims of a miscarriage of justice, other drivers for acceptance filled the vacuum. As discussed, the routine of imprisonment played a role for men who had had several previous sentences, leading to acceptance 'based on habit or routine'. At the same time, the prison environment seemed to induce both 'instrumental/prudential' acceptance and 'constraint-based' acceptance. It was clear that some of the interviewees were aware that not questioning their sentence made their life easier, so in that sense they had an incentive for accepting it (instrumental compliance), but this incentive was not administered by anyone. Instead, it was a result of the way in which the prison experience and human psychology interact, and thus structural constraints also contributed to the sometimes convoluted accounts of acceptance discussed in this chapter. I have termed this (convoluted) type of acceptance *coping-acceptance*, as it was induced by the need to cope with the prison environment, a need which will be less pressing (if present at all) in the context of community sentences. Importantly, others have argued that only normative compliance with community sentences is likely to lead to long-term behavioural change. Robinson and McNeill write:

> whilst an offender might initially comply formally for instrumental reasons ... or because of perceived constraints ... or (perhaps) out of an unthinking habit of deference to legal authority, these kinds of mechanisms alone or in concert are unlikely to be able to yield substantive compliance with the spirit of the order, let alone the kinds of changes required to generate longer-term compliance with the law. (Robinson and McNeill, 2008, p. 440)

If this significance of the different drivers for compliance can be extrapolated to the drivers for the acceptance shown by the interviewees, then in most instances their acceptance of their sentence does not mean that they are less likely to offend in the future. In this sense, irrespective of their acceptance of the sentences, the legitimacy of sentences clearly continues to matter.

5
Narrative Demands and Desistance

Introduction

The previous chapter discussed how the prison environment impacted on the way the men saw their sentence. However, they were not only coping with the prison environment, but also giving prison a place in their life narrative. This equally had consequences for the way they framed their imprisonment and parole. As discussed in detail in Appendix II, narratives both draw on a wider life story, with consequences for identity, and are a situated performance. This chapter discusses how some of the men, by telling a certain story in the interview, were testing out as well as asserting their identity as a non-offender or a reformed character. In doing so, it moves away from the research questions about purpose and fairness, instead attempting to describe how sentences were given meaning in the context of whole lives.

The stories we tell to and about ourselves need not be stable over time. As Josselson (1995) found when interviewing women several times over 20 years, elements that were important in a story at one point disappeared from view later, only to sometimes re-emerge as significant as the interviewees' view of themselves and their life story changed. She writes that 'in understanding ourselves, we choose those factors of our experience that *lead to the present* and render our life story coherent' (Josselson, 1995, p. 35, emphasis added). Presser (2008) makes the further point that narratives do not only concern the past and the present, but also need to make sense of the desired future. Gergen and Gergen (1997) have noted that progressive narratives, ones in which things get better, fulfil an important social function in that they allow us to believe in positive change. They argue that a progressive narrative can be self-reinforcing, because the hope generated in telling this kind of story provides us with motivation to make the projected positive future a reality.

This chapter examines how these narrative demands, as well as those more specific to prisoners, shaped the stories told by the men at the end of their sentence and those on licence, and for some, their view of their imprisonment. As in the previous chapter, the narratives of the former group are discussed first, after which these will be compared and contrasted with the stories told by the men on licence.

Transformation through imprisonment

The very end of a sentence may well be an especially significant point at which to tell the story of one's imprisonment. By then the sentence is almost in the past, and a return to society awaits, leaving the future wide open to narrative possibilities. Despite their strategy of 'keeping their head down' the interviewees' accounts confirmed that prisoners are more likely to think about the world outside at the end (as well as the beginning) of their sentence (Hood and Sparks 1970, cited in Burnett, 2004, p. 156).

> my parole was coming and 'I don't know if I'm getting my parole or not' so I was getting quite excited and time was slowing down again, you know what I mean? (Doug)

The most progressive narrative open to many of the men at the end of their sentence was one in which there had been a change that made future desistance coherent with what had gone before.[1] As Maruna has noted, 'the present "good" of the reformed ex-offender must be explained somehow through biographical events' (2001, p. 85). Several of the men interviewed explained their future desistance through the positive impact imprisonment had had on them; they told a story of transformation through imprisonment.

> Because as I say, I really think things are going to be different this time. Whereas before I have known (.) I have maybe said they're going to be different, but I KNEW. I knew it wasn't like-, but this time things ARE different, eh? Just, it's not a case of thinking it, I KNOW they are different. I don't want to be in this life no more. (Colin)
>
> Makes me, makes me in a good way feel now, looking back, that maybe the best thing was that I have done this sentence, now my eyes are open and I come out with a different attitude and a different aspect and look at things different, you know? And really, to go from

eighteen and now I'm going out, twenty-four, I'm going about with my eyes open, I'm not going to be running about like a daft wee boy, out in the street drinking, stealing cars. (Gordon)

And I've learned from it, you ken what I mean. (.) I'm not coming back to jail again. Definitely not. You see, my other sentences were all small, smallish...Just because they're small ones, you accept them, they're just small, don't have time to come to your senses but now this is a big one, you're confined for so long, plenty of time to think, you ken what I mean, about your past. (James)

These interviewees typically expressed gratitude for their sentence and saw it as a major turning point in their lives. James and Colin even expressed regret that they had not been given a long-term sentence the first time they were imprisoned, which they felt might have allowed them to desist sooner. They told what Presser (2008) has called a 'reform narrative'; one in which moral transformation has taken place. As may be recalled from Chapter 3's section on reform, the men discussed here credited their transformation to different aspects of their experience of imprisonment. Very briefly, Colin attributed the change in his outlook to staff 'taking an interest', Gordon recounted how he had very actively engaged with cognitive behavioural courses and bettered himself by using all the resources available within prison, while James felt that having time to think had allowed him to come to new insights.

These men had found something in their imprisonment that allowed them to 'knife off' their criminal pasts, at least in the way they constructed their narratives during the interview. The slightly odd phrase 'knifing off' was used by Sampson and Laub (2005) to describe how turning points, such as marriage, moving to a new area and military service but, significantly in this context, also stints in reform schools, allowed the offenders in their research to separate their future selves from their past selves. They 'knifed off' their pasts, including social roles and friendships, thus 'providing the opportunity for identity transformation' (Sampson and Laub, 2005, p. 18). The concept of 'knifing off' has been examined in depth by Maruna and Roy (2007), who have pointed out that it more aptly applies to situations where structural changes in people's lives mean that opportunities (both positive and negative) are restricted, rather than to changes in self-perception. They emphasise that any 'knifing off', given the violence inherent in the term, should be definitive. However, they also note that imprisonment, like military service, does knife off connections to opportunities and identities on the outside, albeit temporarily. Perhaps these interviewees were trying to use this temporary freedom from past identities and temptations to construct stories in which their lives *were* irreversibly changed, although whether a definitive break (or cut) with the past had been achieved remained to be seen.

Equally, it may not be so much the 'knifing off' inherent in imprisonment that meant the interviewees ascribed such transformative power to it, as the fact that their prison sentence was the only *possible* fulcrum of change at the time of the interview, given that before they were imprisoned they were still offending. Comfort (2008) also found that ex-prisoners ascribed redemptive and rehabilitative powers to their prison sentence even in the absence of any constructive intervention. In other research projects, mostly evaluations, I have been told similar stories of transformation, but with the transformative power ascribed to peer support upon release from prison or to a cognitive behavioural programme. For example, a programme participant said:

> Your perspective on life is totally out the window, like. Before I started [the course] I couldn't be bothered with anything, get a job, being with my family. And now I've got a job, I am with my family and everything is going brilliant. (Schinkel and Whyte, 2009, p. 51)

And a peer support recipient commented:

> To be honest with you, I don't think I would have been able to do it myself. As I say, I would have probably ended up drinking again and reoffending. (Schinkel, Jardine, Curran, Whyte and Nugent, 2009, p. 41)

It might be that offenders (as well as others with problematic identities, or even anyone dissatisfied with their current situation) are likely to ascribe transformative power to anything that holds the possible promise of fulfilling this role. Given the value of the progressive narrative (Gergen and Gergen, 1997) in explaining and further stimulating positive change, one might be created wherever it is both needed and possible.

A desire for transformation was not only evident in the accounts of those who told a reform narrative. Several others seemed to attempt to construct a similar account, but struggled to maintain it. Like Peter (see Chapter 4), they would start a story in which prison transformed them, but then contradict themselves in other parts of the interview. Doug said, when asked about the meaning of his sentence:

> Eehm (.) the meaning of my sentence, what it is to me? Eeh (.) it makes you think more on part of (.) the value of life a bit more in the

future. Eehm (.) probably helped me think, if I was ever in certain situations I'd think a lot more about my actions (.) and what harm they can cause (.) and what harm they can cause to me as well as anybody else. It would probably make me think a lot more, eh?

But later, he said about his future:

Never say never eh, anything could happen. My victim or anybody else who's got grievances with me might try and attack me, know what I mean, I don't know whether I'll seek revenge after that, know what I mean, I just don't know. (Doug)

Similarly Graham first said:

Aye, I think I've changed, you know what I mean, I really do think I have changed. I think this sentence has opened my eyes up to a lot of things. Just, the way I look at life, stop being selfish, stop thinking about myself all the time. I've got a wee/ I've got a family, I've got a wee girl, you know, I just want to make things different for her, I want to give her an upbringing, a better upbringing than I did, y'know?

But later he was also less optimistic about his chances of going straight.

I hope to get my life sorted, but they can/ they just keep on putting me in hostels/ it's not going to work. Something will happen, I'll do something again, y'know. (Graham)

These quotes suggest that Doug and Graham tried (and would have liked) to tell a story of transformation in prison, but were not quite able to maintain its coherence. In this, they were similar to the 55 per cent of Burnett's (2004) respondents who wanted to desist but were not sure that they would manage to achieve this (with 39 per cent thinking desistance was not even 'probable'). Their interviews also resembled those reported in Giordano et al. (2002) in which the interviewee displayed an openness to change, but because of 'a hedge or a break in the storyline' (p. 1031), did not present a confident account of such change.

What is the difference between those who did maintain the coherence of their desistance throughout the interview and those who did not? First of all, it is possible the difference is an artefact of the interaction. As the interview with Peter discussed in Chapter 4 demonstrates, if I had asked different questions, or pushed harder, James, Colin and Gordon may also have partially discredited their own transformation narrative.

Conversely, if the interview had been shorter, or certain questions had been omitted, Peter, Graham and Doug might have maintained the coherence of their transformation through imprisonment. However, reflecting back on these interviews, and looking at them as a whole, the former three were more invested in their story of change and worked harder to *make* it fit the facts. For example, when Gordon's language slipped at one point so that it allowed for a slight possibility of reoffending by using the word 'hopefully', he immediately corrected this:

> I'm hopefully/ I will manage outside, no, I'm definitely going to do it. (Gordon)

By interrupting himself with 'no, I'm definitely going to do it' he reaffirmed his commitment to his preferred narrative. He seems to be training himself to think in the 'right' way – in the process giving credence to the theory that the narratives we tell ourselves shape our identities and our futures (e.g., Josselson, 1995; Maruna, 2001; McAdams, 2008; Pavlenko, 2002; Singer, 2004).

Equally committed to their transformation narrative, Colin and James worked hard to make a distinction between their current sentence and their previous sentences, which had failed to bring about desistance. Colin did this by emphasising the difference between short-term sentences and long-term sentences throughout his interview, returning to this point at least eight times. Indeed, the very first thing he said when he was asked to tell the story of his sentence was:

> Well, I think this sentence is the only actual one that I have managed to gain stuff out of. I have managed to get myself off the drugs and that. Just there is more sentence manage/ every other sentence I have done, it's been all short term sentences.

The distinctions he drew between his sentences came close to 'splitting' (see Hollway and Jefferson, 2000), with all the negative aspects of imprisonment projected onto his previous (short-term) sentences, which were seen as only harmful, so that the present sentence could be constructed as only positive. James, who had served a sentence of five years before, had to draw a distinction between this and his present sentence.

> I was only in for two and a half years, so I was out pretty quick, two and a half years. I was up in Aberdeen for a year, by the time I moved there was eighteen month left to do, that was me out. And this one, a lot of time to think. (James)

James's need to defend the fairness of his sentence, as discussed in Chapter 4, was most likely also related to the transformative role he ascribed to it in his wider narrative. James's, Colin's and Gordon's narratives were *about* their transformation, the main theme of their story, in a way that Doug's and Graham's narratives were not. Peter's narrative centred around transformation, until he abandoned this in the face of inconsistency, after which he emphasised his victimisation instead.

Why credit imprisonment with transformation?

Burnett and others have found that prisoners who were most certain of their future desistance were likely to be those who faced fewer problems upon release (Burnett, 2004; LeBel et al., 2008). While the men telling me stories of transformation through imprisonment were confident about their desistance, analysis across the interviews revealed that telling this type of narrative was, in fact, a strategy born from a lack of alternatives and resources. Other men were able to construct a positive account without having to tell this type of story. Instead, some told a story in which they had never really been an offender but were led to commit their crime through a combination of circumstances (see Chapter 4). They expected to return to their old existence, so that prison was just a glitch in an otherwise favourable life. While Devan and Robert (one previous sentence, but twenty years ago) were the only ones at the end of their sentence to tell this type of story, others at the start of their sentence did the same. David and Paul, like Devan, had no previous offences, while Alan had served one short-term prison sentence in the past. All of these men identified themselves as 'non-starters' (Burnett, 2004): they said their offending had been out of character and were certain they would not offend again in the future. Accordingly, they were able to tell 'stability narratives', with the narrator 'steady in his propensity to act according to moral principles' (Presser, 2008, p. 62). They had no need for any transformation.

A further factor which seemed to negate the need for a transformation narrative, one which often coexisted with a 'non-starter' identity, was having resources available upon release. Maruna has noted that:

> The white-collar or corporate deviant can fall back on family savings, a college education, or the support of well-connected friends to aid their transition out of crime. (Maruna, 2001, p. 14)

While none of the participants quite fit the bill of white-collar criminals, nonetheless all the men mentioned above (Devan, Robert, David, Paul and Alan) as well as Alex and Dan had resources to overcome the potential negative impact of imprisonment, such as supportive families, savings, well-paying jobs they could return to and stable accommodation.

> Eeehm, and (.) what I'm gonna do is, once I've got all this licence and things out of the way, I'm going to relocate to Canada ... So eehm, I'm kind of lucky, I mean (.) when I was a bit younger, I invested some money in some like flats and stuff in Aberdeen and rented them out, then I was lucky enough to get the timing of it right, you know, I sold before the property bubble burst and stuff, so it's not like, I mean, I have, I have resources to go out to. (Alex)

Accordingly, desistance was a likely prospect for these men, which meant they had no reason to tell a story that revolved around the positive impact of imprisonment. Giordano et al. have also commented that those with the most resources do not have to rely on 'agentic moves' (2002, p. 1026) in order to desist. However, those who had resources but were not able to portray themselves as 'non-starters' did need some explanation of the projected change in their behaviour upon release. Both Alex and Dan explained their future desistance through maturation:

> I shan't be back in jail, because I know that if I come back again, I'm coming back in here to die in jail. Because there is no way, nobody lives forever. And I've already outlived a lot of my peers. (Dan, late 60s)

> I'm 36 now, 37 in April and I can, I can feel in myself a, a, a tapering down of that, of that risk tolerance. With age, I feel now I'm becoming increasingly risk averse. There's a clear link between getting older and (.) a decline in, in, or an increase in risk aversion. And I think, I think personally that that's a hormonal thing, I think that's testosterone linked, you know. ... You know, for example, I can just feel, now, that eehm, that, that my willingness or propensity to commit similar crimes in the future would be really low, you know, really low. (Alex)

The transformation through imprisonment narrative can, then, be a way to meet the need to explain a definitive break with the past in the absence of favourable circumstances upon release. But while those who told or tried to tell this type of story did not have many resources at their disposal, they were not the most disadvantaged or stigmatised amongst the interviewees either. Those with the longest histories of imprisonment, and the least favourable prospects upon release, tended not to try to construct a story in which desistance was a coherent outcome. As discussed in Chapter 3, they were so used to imprisonment that it was no longer aversive and therefore desistance was no longer a (necessary) goal for them.

Perhaps the risk arises here of giving an overly structural explanation of narratives. The number of their offences or their resources on the outside did not *determine* the type of narrative the men told. Neither is the above meant to be a typology. The narratives told were too complex to neatly fit into exclusive groups. The freedom the men had to shape their own narrative, despite these also being shaped by their life circumstances, was demonstrated by Peter, who switched from one type of account to another in response to what happened in the interview. Also, not all the participants at the end of their sentence have been mentioned in the above discussion: Neil was neither a very persistent offender nor resigned to future imprisonment, and had precious few resources to draw upon on his release, but even so did not narrate a story of transformation. My notes summarise his case as:

> has had a long term sentence before, nothing about personal change, except for getting older and hoping that he realises it isn't worth it. Wants to avoid further sentences.

On the other hand, Gordon, who did tell a transformation story, had never been imprisoned before and might therefore equally have appealed to a 'non-starter' identity, especially as he maintained he was innocent. This demonstrates that constructing any narrative remains a creative endeavour, far from wholly determined by circumstances. But narratives, while often associated in the literature with agency and creativity, are created and shaped within the confines of our lives. As we use them to make sense of our circumstances, these circumstances inevitably have an impact on the narratives we tell.

As Josselson (1995) has pointed out, narratives are not fixed for evermore. It was notable that with the exception of Andy on licence, only those at the end of their sentence told a story of transformation that wholly relied on imprisonment. Many of those who were at the start of their sentence or on licence also told a story which aimed to make future desistance a coherent possibility, but the emphasis in most of these stories was not on the prison experience. When prison did play a role, it was more often in combination with other factors such as family ties and relationships. For example, Mark referred to support he had received in prison as changing his outlook, but attributed most of his transformation to the promise he had made in the name of his son and the man he had killed.

> What I got the sentence for, the whole time I spent in prison was that I was gonna actually try at least and better my lifestyle, you know, for not just myself, for my wee boy that passed away, that's not here and the man, that died senseless, you know ... and I made a pact / I made a pact with them both and myself really to try and better my life. (Mark)

For others, their prison sentence played little role in their transformation, with relationships being the main focus (see also Chapter 3).

> It's the girlfriend, y'know, keeping a (.) level head on us and stuff like that, know, but I think it's her basically, it's down to her, you know, trying for a family and stuff. (Smitty)

These men found other biographical events to make their desistance coherent, rather than their imprisonment. But for those coming to the end of their sentence, many of whom had cut themselves off from their families in order to limit their horizons, other possible biographical events will have been scarce; hence the focus on imprisonment. It may be that, once these men are out in the community again, they will choose different, more recent, elements of their experience to make desistance coherent. There was some indication that this may be what happens, but before examining this, it is useful to compare the narratives of those on licence with the hopefulness inherent in the transformation narratives of those at the end of their sentence.

Hard times on licence

Compared to the optimistic picture of their future painted by some of the men at the end of their sentence, with prison as a positive element in their lives, the narratives of many of those on licence were less confident and positive; with their imprisonment either portrayed as neutral or negative. This was in part due to their perception that they were institutionalised, as discussed in Chapter 4, but other factors also played an important role.

Six out of the nine men on licence described how, since they had been released from prison, they had isolated themselves, in a sense perpetuating the separation from society that prison had imposed on them.

> I stay in the house all the time, I mean I just stay out the way of people, I don't hang about with anybody or that anymore. I just stay in the house do my own thing if I can. (Andy)

Aye, even out here. I still don't come out much, if I do come out I come in a taxi or I'm in a motor. (Jack)

One reason for this isolation was a feeling of being under surveillance. The men felt that if they were not careful any misstep would be noted and have grave consequences. Many of them had returned to their own communities, and some had a history with individual police officers, who were also still working in these communities. This led to a feeling that their every move was being watched.

I very rarely leave the house. I'm actually FEARED to leave the house because I'm saying to myself 'what if they do want to get me', what if they just want to go 'oh we'll just get him one last time'. (Lino)

Furthermore, the men keenly felt that being on licence, and their criminal record generally, meant that they would be punished much more harshly than others for any misstep. This meant that they felt especially vulnerable when interacting with others.

'Cause it's always something hanging over your head, know what I mean, so you know you can be recalled for the stupidest things. (Smitty)

It's not like I'm feared to go out, it's just that I don't want to be roped into anybody else's shite outside and I'm the one that has to go to jail for it. 'Cause I'm out on licence. (Jack)

The men's sense of surveillance was not only expressed in their narratives, but also in how they approached the interview. Whereas the men in prison often volunteered information about undetected offending and illicit activities, most of the men on licence were much more wary of disclosing any offending. For example, the following excerpt is from an interview with Tony, who was otherwise happy to answer personal questions:

TONY: I mean we do think at times (.) 'I'm a good runner I'll no get caught' but eh...
MS: Mmm, but hopefully you didn't get caught every time? [Interviewee indicates recorder, not a topic he's happy discussing].

Others had similar reactions or hesitated before answering, generally showing much higher levels of awareness of the potential consequences of their disclosures than those in prison.

This sense of surveillance might not have made much difference to their lives if these men had felt confident in their ability to go straight. However, it is clear from the interviews that many no longer felt in charge of their own destiny in the way that those telling transformation stories within the prison did. They did not express the same level of mastery over their own fate and did not see themselves as able to overcome all obstacles. Instead, like the young offenders in other research, they practiced 'diachronic self-control' (Shapland and Bottoms, 2011, p. 274); they limited their actions in such a way that they were unlikely to face temptations they could not resist. They felt that it would be very easy to get swept up in offending behaviour if they saw their old friends, or were amongst other people, and therefore avoided offending by avoiding these situations.

> It took a long time for me to try and get that in my head that, if I don't stay away from the people I've been associating with, I'm gonna KEEP getting into trouble. (Lino)

> I just stay in the house do my own thing if I can and it's/ for me I find it's the only way to avoid trouble. (Andy)

This pessimism about their own agency was compounded for many of these men by the difficulty they faced in finding work. For some, like Lino and Mark, this was not a priority. They felt that living a crime-free life was enough of an achievement for the time being and therefore felt relatively satisfied with their situation:

> I would like to get to that stage eventually, but I reckon with regards to the way I've been feeling, I'm feeling very institutionalised and kinda withdrawn, (.) to a certain extent from wider society. It will probably take a few year before I would even consider that. (Lino)

> I can still stay in my wee flat, I can pick away, I can still do my own wee thing, you know what I mean. I can come and go as I please, I can/ without upsetting anybody, know what I mean. (Mark)

However, for many of the others, legitimate employment was a necessary marker of progress or a financial necessity, and they accordingly felt very frustrated with their inability to secure this. Some had had temporary jobs or worked cash in hand for people they knew or family members, but none had found long-term steady employment.[2]

The last year I've been out and I've maybe been sitting in the house and I'm pissed off and I'm fed up with everything, can't get a job, you feel as if nothing's going right for you. I just/ I've had me sitting saying to myself 'I feel like being back in the jail the now'. (Jack)

I have been looking [for work] the whole time, yeah, eehm but to be honest I've went through phases where I (.) sometimes, you know you'll get really buzzed up and you'll go to the Job Centre every day for two weeks and then things/ you start getting a bit demoralised and things, you just can't find anything, then you end up just leaving it. (Mohammed)

Prison sentences of over two and a half years are never considered 'spent' in Britain and have to be disclosed whenever requested in job applications or interviews (Rehabilitation of Offenders Act, 1974). As all the men I spoke to had served long-term sentences, which by definition are over four years, all of them faced a lifetime of disclosing their prior offending. This meant that in the process of applying for jobs they were not only 'discreditable' by their offending history, but actually 'discredited' (Goffman 1990, p. 143). Like others with a criminal record (Burnett and Maruna, 2006; Schneider and McKim, 2003), the men felt the stigma of being an ex-offender most keenly when facing potential employers.

See I'm scared to go to a job interview, it's just something/ see bringing up my criminal record in front of people that don't know anything about it, it's actually very (.) it makes me really nervous. I don't like bringing it up, it's as if I get really paranoid thinking that people, you know, they'll think you're a very nice person to start with and then when you mention that they just kinda/ as if like that [shakes his hand dismissively]. (Mohammed)

Andy's case was emblematic of the way difficulties in securing employment influenced narratives. His narrative was the only one of those on licence that relied on imprisonment to deliver the power to desist: as described in Chapter 3, he felt it had given him discipline and greater self-esteem. However, this attribution of change may be as much an indictment of his life after prison, two and a half years in which no further catalysts of or even supports for change had been found, as a reflection on his time in prison. Despite his best efforts to go straight – he went to college but left without qualifications and had applied to numerous jobs – he felt unable to break away from his previous life because his attempts to establish a new identity were coming to nothing. His frustration about this was palpable throughout the interview and he was probably the most despondent of all the interviewees.

> So what's the point of trying to change if there's nothing you can do to move on, you know what I mean, so. I feel kinda bad telling you this, it's just a hopeless cause, [slightly laughing] really, for me, I'm starting to think, it's horrible. I came out with all these big ideas and I went to college, so 'I'm gonna use it' and 'I'm gonna use my experiences, I'm gonna try and change, I'm gonna try and let people know what it could be like in my situation'. Pfff, it just didn't happen man.... Like I was saying, the thing that's really frustrating me the now is not being able to get a job and it's so, so annoying, so frustrating honestly it's just (.) it feels like everything's just wasted, every bit of my sentence, every effort I've made after it just, pffff, been a waste of time that's what it's starting to feel like. Pretty scary. (Andy)

Andy saying 'I feel kinda bad telling you this' indicates that he feels this ending is spoiling his story, the one that should have progressed from making the most of his prison sentence to having the job and life he envisaged. Instead, he is feeling dragged back to his previous life and that 'everything's just wasted', even his transformative prison sentence. His final comment in this quote 'pretty scary' sums up well how he portrayed his life throughout the interview: as careering out of his control. Ironically, he would most likely have told a much more positive story, like Colin, Gordon and James, if he had been interviewed before release. Sometimes, it seems, imprisonment promises endings that the realities of freedom cannot deliver.

One of the ironies contained in the men's accounts was the way in which prison could be more accommodating of a positive identity than freedom. Within prison, the men only compared themselves to other prisoners, all of whom were in the same predicament. Given that staff were generally seen as treating the men with (enough) respect and that there was very little discussion of their offence within the prison, there was actually little stigma experienced within that environment. The combination of the ready availability of work, limited demands, and constraints on what the men *could* aspire to in prison meant that they were generally satisfied with their own achievements within that environment. However, upon release the possibilities for achievement were amplified, and the men were more likely to compare themselves to their peers on the outside, who usually had jobs, steady relationships and children. Partners also tended to be less understanding of the men's situation once they were released, which could cause problems.

> And because... she was working, she was staying with me, the brew has more or less said 'you take her money, you're living off her'. And it's not as easy as that, know what I mean, *that's not the way things go*, so she wasn't having it. Well, she was keeping me going for a couple of months and then she started moaning about the money and it was just, pffff, arguing, so now she's got her own house, and that's it. (Andy, emphasis added)

Andy's girlfriend's perception that 'that's not the way things go' reflects the societal expectation that men are breadwinners, a role that was difficult to fulfil for Andy given his criminal record. With both themselves and their environment expecting more of them, and opportunities to meet these expectations few and far between, being a released ex-prisoner was a more stigmatising experience for most than being a prisoner.

However, this generally down-beat portrayal of life on licence is not to say that there were no positives, even for those who were frustrated by their search for employment. In fact, there were some indications that a few of the men on licence were using the support they received in the community, rather than their prison sentence, as part of an explanation of why they were (going to be) able to desist.

> This is probably about the best I've done since I came out. Out of all of them. I know if I didn't have the support of some people the now I wouldn't have been able to do it, do you know what I mean? (Jack)

> The level of support that [social worker] and [drug worker]'s gave me has been second to none, I've not had anywhere NEAR that kinda help before in the past, so I'm very grateful for the two of them, for what they've done for me. It is still down to me anyway to make the decisions, I suppose, at the end of the day, but without their guidance and help I'd certainly, I think there's a good chance that I'd be back in on drugs or I'd be on something, I'd be involved in something somewhere. (Lino)

Using an element of the present to explain desistance, rather than something that is in the past, may be preferable when there are further problems to be faced. Anything that is firmly in the past will not be able to solve ongoing problems, for example, his prison sentence is not going to solve Jack's difficulties with finding work. As Giordano et al. write: 'such cognitions are eventually grounded in the past (memories of previous jail time) and do little to direct or sustain any kind of forward motion' (2002, p. 1034). But when the transformation is still in progress (for example, through support from social workers), then present problems may still be overcome. Therefore, locating change in the present may facilitate a more hopeful outlook than locating it in the past like Andy. These types of narratives were much more nuanced and less definitive than the prison transformation narratives. As discussed above, Lino and Jack both isolated themselves in order to avoid offending and did not have any ready solutions for the problems they still faced, such as mental health problems (Lino) and unemployment (Jack). They did not exhibit the blind optimism of those who were still in prison and their belief in their desistance was much more tentative. The next section theorises what impact a strongly optimistic narrative might have on desistance, and whether the more nuanced and perhaps more realistic of those on licence will be more or less powerful in facilitating desistance.

The power of transformation narratives

Recent literature has made much of the role of subjective changes, including confidence in one's ability to go straight, in the desistance process (Burnett and Maruna, 2004; Giordano et al., 2002; LeBel et al., 2008; Maruna, 2001; Presser, 2008). In his seminal work, *Making Good*, Maruna (2001) found that ex-offenders who had desisted from crime told a 'redemption script', which contained three elements: an optimism about one's own ability to overcome obstacles, a motivation to contribute to causes greater than oneself and a belief in one's own, essentially good, true self. In contrast, persisting offenders told a 'condemnation script' in which they portrayed themselves as powerless to overcome their problems and therefore 'doomed to deviance' (Maruna, 2001, p. 74). The book strongly suggests that developing a redemption script has a positive impact on the process of desistance. Maruna and co-authors asserted in a later article that 'these narrative patterns seem to distinguish successful from unsuccessful ex-prisoners, *predicting* successful reform after imprisonment' (Maruna, Wilson and Curran, 2006, p. 181, emphasis added).

My results suggest that the connection between optimistic narratives and desistance may also run the other way, with desistance strengthening such narratives. The transformation stories I came across amongst the men at the end of their sentence in some ways resembled the redemption scripts as described by Maruna (2001): those telling them ascribed much power to themselves to overcome obstacles and presented themselves as essentially good in the present. However, it is possible that some of them will be unsuccessful in their move away from crime and will have to give up their transformation story once they have reoffended. Only those who do manage to desist will still tell a story of transformation years later. If the transformation story is a preferred narrative, told by many prisoners who have few resources on the outside but are also not resigned to a life of imprisonment, then it might not be (only) that those who develop redemption scripts desist, but also that those who desist are the ones able to retain their redemption scripts.

To see if this is plausible, if the transformation narratives reported here might become redemption scripts in time, it is necessary to examine their differences as well as their commonalities. An important aspect of redemption scripts is that Maruna's interviewees appealed to an essentially good self – they did not condemn their past self as having been bad, but saw themselves as having been led astray from their essential goodness (Maruna, 2001; see also Presser, 2008; Vaughan, 2007). Many of the men I interviewed, on the other hand, did not disown the acts they had committed or practice neutralisation techniques such as minimising the harm done or their own responsibility (Sykes and Matza, 1957). This may be the consequence of their current imprisonment or ongoing contact with criminal justice social work, both of which are known to emphasise the need to take responsibility for one's offences (Maruna, 2001; McKendy, 2006; Miller, 2011). If this is the case, then their acknowledgement of responsibility and previous 'badness' may well be tempered for successful desisters as crime recedes in the past and contact with criminal justice agencies reduces. This difference, then, does not mean that transformation stories cannot turn into redemption scripts over time. This is supported by a recent retrospective study examining the identity formation of reformed ex-prisoners (Aresti, Eatough and Brooks-Gordon, 2010). For some of these desisters, defining moments of change had taken place in prison. Aresti et al. write:

> It is at this point that the first signs of self-change begin to emerge, as the men move towards taking control of their lives and they attempt to create a new and meaningful identity. (2010, p. 175)

The fact that at least some of these men, who otherwise tell something much like a redemption script, see a personal transformation in prison as the cradle of their new identity makes it plausible that if James, Gordon and Colin manage to desist, their stories may come to resemble those of Maruna's (2001) desisters.

An important tenet of my research is that the narrative one prisoner tells is not set in stone. I have noted above that those who tell a 'transformation through imprisonment narrative' in the present may have to abandon it if they reoffend. Equally, reality might come to contradict this story in more subtle ways, as it did for Peter in the course of the interview. Because he could not maintain the coherence of the distinction between this and previous sentences, he abandoned his transformation story and went on to construct something much more like Maruna's persisters' condemnation scripts, in which his offending was a product of his youth in institutions and he was condemned to commit further crimes. Those coming to the end of a (long) prison sentence are still able to choose between the different scripts, because their reality is not yet one that can either confirm or disprove whether they will desist or not. Those trying to tell a transformation story did support this with reference to their behaviour in the prison, in terms of staying away from drugs or avoiding confrontation, but with most everyday frustrations and temptations into crime 'knifed off' for the time being, they are in principle able to tell either story, or a combination of both, or different ones on different days or to different audiences. In that sense, both the meaning of their prison sentence and their possible futures are not yet fixed.

On the other hand, it is possible (and maybe even probable) that those who told a transformation story *will* be more likely to desist than those who tried and failed, because their narratives suggest or signal their commitment to this goal. Several studies have attempted to unravel the contribution of subjective factors to desistance. In a prospective study Burnett (2004) found that the more confident about desistance imprisoned property offenders were when they came to the end of their sentence, the less likely they were to have reoffended up to 20 months after release. However, those who were the most confident about their desistance also had the fewest problems facing them upon release. A later quantitative study using the same data combined with ten-year reconviction data, aimed to separate the effect of social problems from the effect of subjective factors (LeBel et al., 2008). It found that (the number of) social problems faced upon release had the greatest impact on whether desistance was achieved, but that (1) the perception that being an ex-offender would make desistance difficult, (2) identifying oneself as a 'family man' and (3) regretting past offending also had some impact. The level of confidence in one's ability to desist only impacted on eventual desistance through reducing the number of social problems upon release (although an alternative explanation, acknowledged but not tested by this study, is that expectations of social problems upon release made the offenders in this study less confident of their eventual desistance). When these findings are applied to Colin, James and Gordon, it would appear that they should have little advantage over others as they did face multiple problems upon release, including unemployment, being housed in a hostel or with parents and financial difficulties, issues their transformation story had no power to resolve. LeBel et al.'s findings also suggest that those men who credited their transformation to their children rather than to imprisonment might have a better chance of desisting, as the identity of 'family man' had a greater impact than confidence about desistance.

Giordano et al. (2002) took a different approach to separating out the effects of structural and subjective changes. They interviewed 127 delinquent girls and 127 delinquent boys in 1982 and then interviewed 85 per cent of these now young adults again in 1995. Besides more structured questions, they also conducted narrative interviews with 97 of the women and 83 of the men at the second sweep. They found that structural variables, such as employment and high quality marriages (rated as such by the respondents) did not significantly predict desistance, partly because under contemporary circumstances, jobs are not offered, but rather obtained with great difficulty, and marriage has become increasingly uncommon. Given these circumstances, they argue, offenders *need* a real openness to change before any change can happen. Because structural changes do not fall in their lap, offenders have to work hard to leave their old lives behind. Giordano et al. write:

> At the point of change, this new lifestyle will necessarily be 'at a distance' or a 'faint' possibility. Therefore, the individual's subjective stance is especially important during the early stages of the change process. (Giordano et al., 2002, p. 1000)

However, they also note that some of their respondents lived in such deprived circumstances that even the most strong-willed and motivated might not manage to desist. They argue that, while openness to change is necessary, it is not sufficient. It needs to be accompanied by 'hooks for change', which will allow the person to turn their wish into a reality. Interestingly, for some of their respondents imprisonment provided this hook. Giordano et al. note, however, that the prison experience might not be as good a 'hook for change' as others, such as religion and parenthood, because it neither provides a blueprint for life after imprisonment nor a new identity to replace the old one of offender (see also Maruna and Roy, 2007).

Giordano et al.'s findings have implications for the power of the transformation story as told by James, Colin and Gordon. On the one hand, those who tell a transformation story may be more likely to desist than those who are less committed to a changed life, but their use of prison as a fulcrum of change might not be as powerful as other possible hooks they might have used to construct their narratives, had they been available. For example, if they had found religion in prison, this may have been a more powerful predictor of desistance. As it is, they still have to leave prison and find a new way of living on the outside, rather than stepping into a ready-made identity (and, in the case of religion, a ready-made community). This may be another reason why the men on licence tended to credit other aspects of their experience with their transformation, such as becoming a father, or realising that they needed to be there for their children. This may have provided them with better 'hooks for change'. And, again, James, Colin and Gordon might well shift the attribution of their transformation from prison to more suitable 'hooks' once (or if) they encounter these.

A further implication of the Giordano research for my findings is the way in which the importance of subjective changes is determined by resources. As those with the most resources are unlikely to need much motivation to escape their pasts and those with the fewest are unlikely to escape it at all, the authors emphasise that 'on a continuum of advantage and disadvantage, the real play of agency is in the middle' (Giordano et al., 2002, p. 1026). The question is whether Colin, James and Gordon will have sufficient resources and encounter enough opportunities to fit into this 'middle' and to make their desistance a reality. While my research was not longitudinal and it is not possible to say whether their accounts will come to closely resemble those of the men on licence once they are released, the latter's accounts do describe possible ways of navigating (and narrating) the world after release. As discussed above, in many ways the men on licence were further from telling a redemption-like script than Colin, James and Gordon. They were less confident about their ability to control their own behaviour, less optimistic about the future and those who wanted to find work were more frustrated with their situation. On the other hand, all were still on licence and most were actively trying to avoid offending by staying away from the situations in which they thought this might be likely. In addition, some of their stories had in common with redemption scripts that they attributed at least part of their decision and ability to desist to significant others and criminal justice staff. Despite all the obstacles, they were managing to live in the real world without offending (or at least, without committing the kind of offences for which they would have been recalled).

Perhaps, the lack of zeal on the part of many of the men on licence reflects what has been called the 'zig-zag' path of desistance, where motivation to stop offending waxes and wanes according to circumstances and inclination, and which includes stumbles and relapses along the way (Burnett, 2004; Maguire and Raynor, 2006; Piquero, 2004; Taxman, Young and Byrne, 2004). There might not be one 'point of change' as suggested by Giordano et al. (2002).[3] Instead, there might be one *first* moment of change, the first time a person decides to aim for desistance, followed by many re-affirmations later after periods of less certainty. If so, it is likely that in the development from prospective transformation story to retrospective redemption script a period in which the storyline is less certain is to be expected, until the person either reoffends or attains the position he envisioned originally. This may also reflect the difference (and the period) between primary and secondary desistance (Maruna and Farrall 2004, cited in McNeill, 2006, p. 47), while at the same time problematising the order in which these occur. While those who told a transformative account at the end of their sentence claimed a newly created non-offender identity (the first inkling of secondary desistance), in all likelihood they would have to go through a period, like those on licence, where the future would be less certain, despite (hopefully) an increasing period of non-offending (primary desistance). Aresti (2010) has written of this in-between stage, which he calls 'life in transition' that

> the men's successful attainment of early goals appeared to induce feelings of competency and confidence, and had a positive impact on their sense of self, motivating them to engage in more challenging pro-social pursuits. (p. 135)

This attainment of goals may be what is missing for the men I spoke to on licence. They had not met with much early success, and so for them their continued desistance (an absence of a behaviour, rather than an active involvement in something new) was the only marker of change. It is telling that none of these men, most of whom had been out of prison for at least two years, felt they had attained their desired life and identity.

Most were still waiting for the structural changes that would allow them to secure a happy ending. If these changes do not occur, then their desistance might not be the redemptive journey described by Maruna as 'making good' (2001), but one that ends in their current situation: one in which they are trying to maintain an everyday existence on the outside without offending, by 'knifing off' most of the social world.

Conclusion

This chapter has discussed how narrative demands shaped the stories told by the interviewees and how different stories might be related to different types of outcomes. In relation to my original research questions, the main contribution of this chapter is that it is not only the immediate need of coping with a long-term sentence, discussed in the last chapter, but also the longer-term need of constructing a story that makes sense of their lives that influenced the interviewees' views of (the legitimacy of) their imprisonment. When a sentence is constructed as 'the best thing that could have happened' it is unlikely that it will at the same time be experienced as unfair. Similarly, in such a narrative the sentence is almost inevitably positioned as reformative.

This chapter has also examined the ways in which people's lives and the way they make sense of their sentence interact. Some pasts lend themselves better to certain kinds of stories and, conversely, different types of stories might be associated with different futures. Amongst the men I spoke to, it was those with few resources and a significant criminal history who were most likely to position their prison sentence as transformative just before their release. They occupied the middle position amongst the interviewees, with those with few previous offences and/ or good resources seeing themselves as not in need of transformation in order to desist, whereas those with long histories of institutionalisation and sentences tended not to see desistance as a goal. A large part of this chapter has been dedicated to the question of whether telling a transformation story is, in fact, likely to make transformation a reality. The evidence suggests that, if optimism and confidence in one's ability to desist has any predictive power, it is modest, especially if this confidence is based on the transformative power of one's prison sentence, as this does not provide any blueprint or identity for life after imprisonment. The problems the lack of such a blueprint leads to were clear in my interviews with the men on licence, very few of whom had been able to build up an alternative life and identity, instead isolating themselves to protect their non-offending.

Is such a life of isolated desistance enough? Other researchers have found that desistance does not necessarily involve a grand narrative arc, ending in redemption. Most of Appleton's (2010) interviewees on life licence had no ambition to move beyond their 'normal' lives into contributing to society in a particularly meaningful way. A few (mostly sex offenders) had failed to overcome the stigma associated with their offence and led bleak lives. Appleton writes:

> Far from becoming 'wounded healers' or 'moral heroes' these respondents often faced a menial and lonely existence. They described enduring many desperate and monotonous periods in their lives. (p. 167)

Similarly, there are tentative findings that the concept of 'making good' by giving back to society at large has no relevance for French desisters, who tended to concentrate on themselves and their families rather than on others (Herzog-Evans, 2011a). However, while we should not insist on grand ambitions to change the world before desistance is recognised, it also seems wrong to dampen the expectations of those leaving prison in such a way that they no longer aspire to anything beyond mere desistance, such as employment. Admittedly, with income deprivation levels of almost 25 per cent and employment deprivation levels amongst those of working age almost 20 per cent in the areas where interviews with the men on licence took place,[4] finding work as someone who has served a long-term prison sentence is currently very difficult. And tellingly, it was those who did not aspire to employment who were the most content with their situation on licence. But encouraging people to give up the hope of employment is depriving them of a primary good. 'Excellence in work (including a sense of mastery)' has been theorised to be one of the goods that offenders try to reach through offending (Tony Ward and Maruna, 2007; Tony Ward and Marshall, 2007). Encouraging ex-prisoners to stop aspiring to such goods may therefore support desistance, but not a form of desistance that leads to a fulfilling life; arguably it is encouraging them to accept a life less meaningful. While some measure of excellence of work or a sense of making a contribution may be achieved through voluntary work (see Burnett and Maruna, 2006), such voluntary work is unlikely to be ex-prisoners' long-term goal: we all like to be rewarded for the work we do and for most desisters paid work is an essential alternative source of income to crime (LeBel et al., 2008). Moreover, legitimate, interesting and well-paying employment is exactly the kind of thing that can provide the basis for a new identity, one that can come to replace the offender identity that the interviewees were trying to leave behind. Employment is the basis of a daily routine for most people (Bushway and Apel, 2012), allows them to earn a living, is more highly evaluated in our culture than unpaid work, provides the opportunity for social contact and many people derive a large part of their identity from the professional roles they fulfil (Watson, 1996), while unemployment leaves large swathes of time without any purpose. By not doing much of anything (not working, not studying) and staying away from most things, the men I interviewed on licence did not lead the kind of life that was likely to fulfil them in the long term. Certainly, they did not feel that their story had reached a satisfactory ending. At the time of the interviews, they were practicing ritualism (Merton, 1938): they had given up on the goal of personal success and a sense of mastery so that they could stay within the law. There is a danger that the frustration many felt as a consequence might lead to (a return to) innovation, or finding non-legitimate ways to reach their goals (ibid.); they might decide to aim for a measure of (financial) success or admiration from others even if this means a return to offending. Might it, in the end, be those who do find more suitable hooks for change and realise some early goals, thereby moving towards 'making good', at least in their own eyes, who will manage to sustain desistance?

6
Conclusion

Introduction

In response to a gap in the literature and a lack of connection between normative theories and lived experience, this book has examined how long-term prisoners make sense of their sentence. This concluding chapter draws the findings together and considers to what extent they are likely to have a bearing on other settings and groups of prisoners. To recap, the questions which the research sought to address were:

- What meanings do offenders give to their sentences? Do any of these meanings align with normative theories? How are these meanings ascribed?
- Do offenders' accounts indicate that any of the stated aims of punishment are achieved?
- What unintended meanings and consequences do sentences have for offenders?
- Do offenders see their sentences as justified? Why (not)? What implications does this have?
- Does the way prisoners see their sentence change as they progress through their sentence?

The final sections of this chapter discuss implications of the findings for current criminal justice policy and practice.

Meaning and normative theories

The connections and divergences between the interviewees' accounts and normative theories were considered in Chapter 3. It described how in their discussions of their sentences, the interviewees' views of their purposes most often aligned with consequentialist justifications of punishment, in particular reform, rehabilitation and deterrence. These purposes of sentencing played a larger role in their accounts than others, because desistance was almost universally desired, and if rehabilitation, reform or deterrence were achieved, a life away from crime would follow (see also Comfort, 2008; Giordano et al., 2002). Incapacitation and punishment, on the other hand, have no consequences beyond the end of the sentence, and were therefore less important to the men.

Despite the desire for rehabilitation and reform, most of the men felt these had not been achieved. Reformative efforts by the prison were seen as overly relying on cognitive behavioural courses, attendance of which was required for progression to lower levels of risk classification and to the open estate (see also Crewe, 2009). The findings suggested that making courses compulsory in this way limited substantive engagement (Robinson and McNeill, 2008), even amongst the men who were initially motivated to attend. What the men wanted was reformative input tailored to them as individuals, rather than the current approach, which they felt treated them as one of many. This view mirrored the 'New Penology' argument (Feeley and Simon, 1992) that managerialist approaches mean that prisoners are treated as mere instances of an aggregate. This was the aspect of their experience of which the men were most critical: being treated as a 'cog in a wheel' made many feel belittled and angry. These feelings were intensified by a perceived lack of rehabilitative effort made on their behalf: many of the men at the end of their sentence faced being released without accommodation or into hostels. This finding, though, will have been in part a consequence of interviewing men who were released directly from a long-term prison, rather than from the open estate.

The men on licence I spoke to had all secured suitable accommodation, and most were full of praise for their case managers, with whom they had very positive and constructive relationships. However, as discussed in Chapter 5, the main stumbling block in their rehabilitation was gaining employment, an area in which their criminal justice social workers seemed powerless to help. The men who did feel reformed often attributed this not to the sentence, but to moments of insight, comments from their family, or having made the effort themselves. It tended to be those who told a narrative that revolved around the transformative power of their prison sentence who attributed their reform to attributes of the prison regime, although the specifics varied. Some of the men mentioned being deterred, but descriptions of the pains of imprisonment were always in tension with the dominant view of prison life as being too easy. This view was partly due to a need to perform masculinity within the prison, but the need to adapt and cope will also have limited the deterrent effect of long-term imprisonment. For many of the men, prison's main deterrent was missing out on life outside, a prospect that started to weigh more heavily as they aged.

Unintended meanings and consequences

The section above has focused on those points where the interviewees' accounts and normative theories of punishment overlapped. But in truth, the *overall* meaning of the sentence was often much more complex and individual. In Chapter 5, I discussed the accounts in which the true meaning of imprisonment went beyond reform or rehabilitation; in which imprisonment was positioned as the fulcrum of change on which the men's future depended. In other accounts, briefly discussed, imprisonment was a routine occurrence, not worthy of further reflection, or even a form of respite. Further meanings have received little attention in the body of this book, but some can be gleaned from the narrative vignettes in Appendix I. While many of the idiosyncratic meanings ascribed to imprisonment were positive (prison has saved me, or has let me avoid a worse fate), some of the men took a darker view, such as prison meaning losing the best years of one's life (Doug) or being dislocated into a gritty drama (Devan).

In contrast, the unintended consequences of imprisonment were almost exclusively negative. Most of the negative consequences were not perceived by those at the end of their sentence and only emerged in the interviews with the men on licence. This was especially true of the institutionalisation they described, discussed in Chapter 4. While the men at the end of their sentence were generally proud of the way they had been able to adapt to imprisonment, the men on licence described paying the price for having cut off relationships, for not having had any responsibility and for having adapted to a strict routine while in prison. Having adapted to being locked in at night and 'keeping themselves to themselves', many described isolating themselves in their homes after release. The reality of life after release furthermore left them less optimistic about their ability to go straight than many of those who were still in prison. The only way they felt they could continue to desist was by avoiding all situations in which they might be tempted or provoked, or practicing what Shapland and Bottoms have called 'diachronic self-control' (2011, p. 274). One of the main obstacles to a more fulfilling form of desistance was the men's inability to secure a job. This high-lights another negative consequence of imprisonment: the stigma of the criminal record. In current economic conditions the requirement to disclose their offending history effectively blocked the men's opportunities to achieve markers of success and to create new identities.

The 'fairness' of sentences

One of the most notable findings of this book, discussed in Chapter 4, is that very few of the men opposed their sentence despite protesting their innocence, feeling their sentence was inconsistent with those of others, seeing the law they had offended against as wrong, or maintaining that the court did not have the moral standing to judge them. While some accepted their sentence for normative reasons, including the level of harm they had caused, I have argued that many of the men's acceptance was driven by other factors. The complex nature of these factors is shown in Figure 6.1 below, in a model of the drivers of acceptance and some of their long-term consequences.

In the rectangles on the bottom left are the considerations mentioned by the interviewees themselves. They referred to their expectations, their guilt or otherwise and the level of harm they had caused in explaining their view of their sentence as fair (or very occasionally as unfair). They also justified their sentence with reference to their general guilt (of other or future offences) and their having broken the law. Especially, the references to general guilt raised more questions than they answered, as did the limited impact of reasons to find the sentence unfair (innocence in particular) on overall evaluations of fairness. In order to answer the questions raised (for example, why would someone justify their sentence with reference to offences not yet committed, why would someone say their sentence is fair when they maintain they are innocent), I identified two main drivers of acceptance of one's sentence that function independently of the particulars of the case or the match between crime and punishment. In Chapter 4, I have discussed how, for the men at the end of their sentence, adapting to the prison environment led to a strategy of limiting their horizons, which was facilitated by a lack of opposition to the sentence. This is represented in the model by the circles on the bottom right. Not questioning one's sentence was seen as making the years in prison easier to bear, as it, along with other ways of limiting thoughts of the outside world, made time pass faster and confronted the men less often and less deeply with what they were missing. The significant impact of the

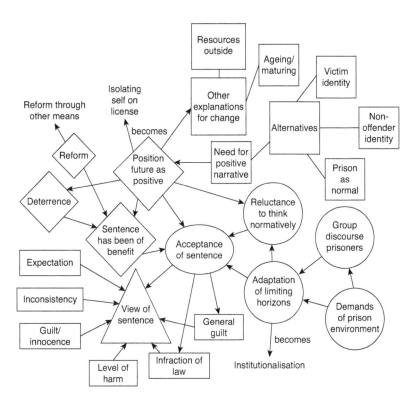

Figure 6.1 Factors in long-term prisoners' views of their sentence

need to cope on the men's evaluation of their sentence has led me to label this type of acceptance as *coping-acceptance*.

In Chapter 5, I have described the impact of narrative needs, represented in the model by the squares at the top of Figure 6.1. The need for a positive narrative meant for many of the men that they had to explain a change from offending in the past to a future of desistance. For some this did not have an impact on their view of their sentence, as they explained change through maturation or having resources outside prison (family support, savings and/or a legitimate job). Others did not try to explain a future of desistance, whether because they felt they had never been 'real offenders', because imprisonment was a normal fact of life, or because this narrative became incoherent within the interview, as it did for Peter, who thereafter appealed to a victim identity. However, others at the end of their sentence tried to explain their desistance through the deterrent, or more usually, the reformative effect of their sentence. Like other imprisoned research respondents (Ashkar and Kenny, 2008; Comfort, 2008) they told a story of 'as if' reform – reform in the absence of significant intervention on the part of the prison regime. Ascribing the outcome of desistance to their sentence meant that they had to position the sentence as a positive within their narrative rather than opposing it as unfair. Interestingly, amongst the men on licence there were very few who attributed their reform to their imprisonment. Instead, they credited it to themselves exclusively, or to the comments made by a family member, usually a child, while acknowledging significant help of others, including criminal justice social workers.

The answer to the question 'do offenders see their sentence as justified?' then, is a complicated one. The men I spoke to on the whole would probably have agreed with a survey item asking this question, but even this is not certain. The difficulty is in the word 'justified'. The interviewees justified the sentence to themselves in different ways, but as this was a strategy borne out of the demands of the prison environment and in some cases their life narrative, this does not mean their sentence 'is justified'. Using Beetham's (1991) conception of legitimacy, I have argued that their consent does not render their sentence legitimate, because the laws the sentences were based upon often did not align with the men's own moral views and in several cases the process and decisions involved had broken the rules that should govern the criminal justice system, such as consistency.

The further question of 'what are the implications of perceptions of (in)justice?' cannot be answered conclusively on the basis of this book. Theory has suggested that perceptions of unfairness are likely to lead to defiance and further offending (Sherman, 1993). But there was no sense that the few men who did oppose their sentence (Devan, Stephen and Alan) were more likely to reoffend. If anything, Devan and Alan were probably more likely than most to desist, because they both appealed to a non-offender identity and had resources to make a law-abiding life in the community likely. It might be that the resources and characteristics that enable people to tell a story of opposition to long-term imprisonment are the same as those that facilitate desistance. If opposition does not predict recidivism, in Chapter 4 I have argued that, conversely, acceptance does not predict desistance. Because the men's acquiescence in their sentence was driven by instrumental and structural reasons, it is unlikely to lead to long-term behavioural change (see also Robinson and McNeill, 2008). The men who told a story of transformation within prison and thereby actively embraced their sentence as the fulcrum for their reform, might be more likely to desist because of their commitment to this goal, but, as discussed in Chapter 5, the predictive power of this type of narrative might be less than sometimes assumed. They will probably need to find other 'hooks for change' and take successful steps towards a new identity in order to make desistance a reality.

How meanings are ascribed

In the section above, I have already discussed the two major influences on the meanings the men ascribed to their sentence: the prison environment and the story they wanted to tell about their lives. In the findings chapters other influences have also been identified. The collective discourse (Miller and Glassner, 1997) among prisoners drove both critical understandings and acceptance. In Chapter 3, I argued that some of the men I spoke to privately held positive views of cognitive behavioural courses, but felt they had to also pay lip-service to the received group discourse that these courses were just an attempt by the prison regime to impress the government or the wider public. At the same time, the apparent lack of critical understandings of the criminal justice system in the group discourse in the prison (see also Crewe, 2009) meant that the men were not stimulated by others to examine their sentence in such terms. Furthermore, the adaptation technique of limiting horizons and thereby accepting the sentence was shared and recommended between prisoners.

The influence of other prisoners on the meanings given to the sentence might well be more pronounced because family contact was often minimised in order to make the sentence easier to bear, and the men often reported feeling they could not share their problems with their families, for fear of worrying them. The views of family members and other loved ones therefore might have had less impact on the meaning-making process than would have otherwise been the case. Family support did have an impact on the meanings ascribed, however, as did other resources the men felt they could draw upon after their release. Where these were significant and made desistance likely, the men were unlikely to present themselves as having radically changed during their sentence. As Giordano et al. (2002) have pointed out, agency is less significant in the desistance process for people who are relatively advantaged.

As discussed elsewhere, criminal justice actors, including the judge, had little impact on the way the men I spoke to made sense of their sentence (Schinkel, in press-a). The only instances where criminal justice actor input was found to have an influence involved some of the men taking on the language of the cognitive behavioural courses in defining their own problems and using the term 'institutionalised' because of their contact with criminal justice social workers after release. In neither case did this input shape their view of the sentence as a whole. Instead, it was the prison environment, their circumstances outside and their desired future that had the greatest effect on how the men made sense of their sentence.

Change over time

The meaning the men ascribed to their sentence did not seem to change appreciably after release, as the men on licence tended not to re-evaluate their sentence spontaneously. They lived on with a sense that their sentence had been fair (enough). However, the way they responded to the different factors leading to acceptance changed, and this partly explains the difference in tone of the interviews with the two groups of men, with the men before release generally being optimistic while those on licence spoke more bleakly. Above, I have identified the institutional pressure of coping with imprisonment and the narrative pressure of telling a progressive story as the two main influences on the men's narratives. Before release, these pressures converged (along with others factors, such as the group discourse amongst prisoners) for some of the men in that they both led to a story of acceptance (or even a welcoming) of the sentence. On licence, however, adapting to the prison environment had come to mean institutionalisation, rather than a chosen strategy to be proud of. At the same time, the need for a progressive narrative still demanded that the men's lives improved. Now institutionalisation combined with the stigma of having a criminal record and the economic recession to counteract progress, as illustrated in Figure 6.2.

Instead of the future the men desired, which for almost all of those on licence included a meaningful and legitimate job, most of the licensees isolated themselves in order to cope with the consequences of their prior adaptation to imprisonment and with the dissonance between their narrative needs and their socio-economic realities. The convergence of forces that brought about acceptance at the end of the sentence (in ovals in Figure 6.2) was temporary – on licence the need to survive the prison environment and the need to have a progressive narrative had come to oppose each other (in rectangles). This did not lead the men to re-evaluate their sentence spontaneously, but men like Andy had started to re-evaluate the possibility of a progressive narrative within the context of their specific lives and were close to giving up. What will happen when these men do decide to throw in the towel is, in the best

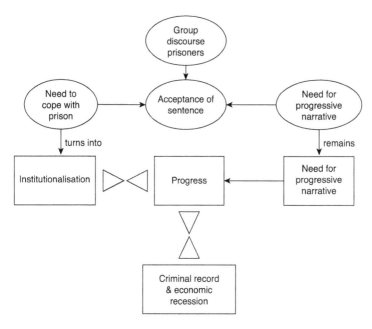

Figure 6.2   Convergence becomes opposition

case scenario, a life of isolation and withdrawal, and in the worst case scenario, a return to offending.

The discussion here is based on a comparison of two different groups of men. This means that the difference in tone in the accounts solicited could be a result of differences between the groups, rather than due to the stage of the sentence. I have attempted here to make the latter theoretically plausible, but future longitudinal research with men before and after release from long sentences should be able to both test the theoretical links I have proposed and to advance our understanding of how meanings change. By focusing on the differences in the accounts told by individuals over time, far more detailed changes will be apparent than in this research, where only differences so marked that they (seemed to) exist between groups of people could be noted and described.

Generalisability

The above sections have brought together my results and made links between different parts of the book. Narrative research methods, and qualitative research in general, are not usually associated with attempts to generalise findings from a sample to a population (Armour, Rivaux and Bell, 2009; Polkinghorne, 2007). This book has instead been concerned with theoretical generalisation: finding concepts to build theories that might generalise to other settings. This section is an attempt to assess to what extent the conclusions reached here are likely to hold for other prisoners elsewhere.

Some of the findings clearly apply to other settings, as research conducted in different prisons and at different times has led to similar results. There was significant agreement between the findings reported here and those arising from Crewe's research in an English prison that held both short-term and long-term prisoners, including opposition to cognitive behavioural courses and a desire for greater individual attention. This suggests that some of the conditions of modern imprisonment, including the lack of individual rehabilitation, are alike across UK prisons. Some of my results have been echoed by research further removed from mine, both in time and place. For example, the finding that the interviewees often limited contact with family in order to make their imprisonment easier to bear resembles results reported by Farber in 1944 (cited in Cohen and Taylor, 1972, p. 71), but not more recent findings with imprisoned women (Bosworth, 1996) and young men on remand or awaiting sentencing (Harvey, 2005). However, for the latter the ties with family were still tight and recently disrupted by imprisonment. At the remand stage, prisoners' main concern is also likely to be the upcoming trial, rather than coping with a long stretch of imprisonment, which might be easier with limited family contact. For the women interviewed by Bosworth (1996) family ties were crucial to their identity in ways that they were not for the interviewees described in this book. The desirability of family contact might therefore depend on the stage of imprisonment and gender.

Other findings are likely to be more specific to the research context. Some landmark studies have focused on the different experiences of people in different prisons (Kruttschnitt and Gartner, 2005; Liebling, 2004; Sparks et al., 1996) and found that prison conditions and staff–prisoner relationships are especially important in determining the experience of the sentence. As noted in the introduction, the prison in which I interviewed men at the end of their sentence has been praised for the positive relationships between staff members and prisoners and for the low levels of violence within the prison. The men I spoke to were also mostly positive about the regime and described the place as a 'fast prison', because their time was filled with activities, meaning it passed more quickly. The finding that many of the interviewees accepted their sentence as part of a wider adaptation might well be a consequence of this type of regime. Very strict and punitive regimes are associated with more oppositional coping styles (Kruttschnitt and Gartner, 2005). Research has also suggested that prisoners in other contexts do take oppositional stances towards the justice system as a whole, and their own treatment in particular, as a result of their imprisonment (Franke et al., 2010; Presser, 2008). It may be only in prisons where conditions are sufficiently favourable that limiting one's horizons to the prison walls is not in itself painful that accepting one's sentence is part of the easiest way to get through the sentence. The studies highlighting opposition referred to above (Franke et al., 2010; Kruttschnitt and Gartner, 2005; Presser, 2008) have all been conducted in the US, where gang membership and ethnic divides lead to higher levels of violence amongst prisoners and where prison regimes tend to rely more on coercion than on legitimacy in order to maintain order (Crewe, 2009). A study by Liebling et al. (2011) of staff–prisoner relationships in HMP Whitemoor provides a useful comparator within the UK (Schinkel, in press-b). Whitemoor is a high security prison holding long-term prisoners, where prisoners are subjected to far greater security measures than the interviewees. The study found that Whitemoor prisoners were searched every time there was prisoner movement within the prison, had to change cells every 28 days and that CCTV cameras were used throughout the prison. The prisoners reported feeling constantly monitored by the regime and staff, even in the interview setting. Staff–prisoner relationships in Whitemoor were furthermore found to be very stigmatising, with staff treating prisoners only as risks to be managed, rather than as individuals. Significantly, many Whitemoor prisoners saw themselves as victims of an unfair criminal justice system and were appealing their sentence. While the interviewees talked of narrowing their lives down to a point where the prison was their whole world, in Whitemoor long-term prisoners preferred to forget that they were in prison, using phrases such as 'taking my head out of jail', 'life transcends the prison' and 'it's like you've been released' (Liebling et al., 2011, p. 48). The discrepancy with the interviewees' phrases of 'keeping your head in the jail', 'not putting your head over the fence' and 'keeping your head down' could not be more striking. In the prison where I conducted my interviews, life was generally portrayed as pretty comfortable, whereas in Whitemoor even the prison building was seen as hostile. Again, it seems likely that it was the relatively liveable environment in the prison that meant that the best strategy was to forget about everything else and therefore to accept one's sentence. In Whitemoor, where prisoners spoke of being afraid of losing their identity because they had to monitor themselves constantly in order to avoid transgressions of the rules, the preferable strategy seems to have been one of mental escape and opposition. Like the interviewees described here, they had to survive the prison environment and try to hold on to some positive sense of self, but within different conditions that made adopting a victim identity the best way to do both these things at once.

These putative interactions between the prison environment and the meaning-making process suggest interesting linkages between the work on prison regimes and the findings reported here. While it is perhaps unsurprising that prisoners living under more favourable conditions generally rate their sentence more positively, it would be interesting to explore whether this is, indeed, due to a pressure to accept the sentence under more favourable conditions, as suggested here. Further research should explore whether more 'moral' prisons (Liebling, 2004) do in fact encourage an adaptation of accepting one's sentence and limiting one's world to the prison more than less 'moral' prisons and what impact this has on the subsequent adaptation to freedom and later desistance. This seems particularly important given the findings in this study that certain kinds of in-prison adaptation can turn out to be counterproductive after release.

The above discussion shows that the prison experience can be very different for male long-term prisoners incarcerated in different prisons. For other groups, such as short-term or female prisoners, the interaction between the prison environment and narrative demands is likely to differ even further. For example, as female prisoners tend to have more childcare responsibilities and a stronger link with their children than imprisoned men (Bosworth, 1996), they may find it much more difficult to forget the outside world and to limit their horizons, even where prison conditions are relatively favourable. As suggested by the interviewees, short-term prisoners are unlikely to need to adapt to the prison environment to the same extent, and may therefore oppose their sentence more easily. But while the specific outcomes may differ, narrative needs and the demands of the environment are likely to be factors in the meanings prisoners ascribe to their sentence.

Widening horizons

One of the main findings discussed in Chapter 4 was that interviewees limited their horizons in prison to make coping easier. It also discussed how adapting to imprisonment in this way had made returning to wider society more difficult for the men on licence. In this concluding chapter, this coping strategy has been linked to the relatively positive prison regime experienced by my interviewees. This raises the possibility that when prisons get most things right, including the safety of prisoners and positive relationships with staff, they have to do more to keep their prisoners' horizons as wide as possible throughout their incarceration. Maintaining relationships with friends and family is especially important in this respect, given the impact on recidivism that positive relationships have (for example Bosworth, 1996; Cullen, 1994; Forste et al., 2011; Mills and Codd, 2008; Social Exclusion Unit, 2002) and the difficulties in reassuming family roles described by the men on licence. The findings discussed in Chapter 4 suggest that two obstacles need to be overcome: the painfulness of contact that is unsuccessful (in the case of unanswered phone calls and letters) or disappointing, and the thinning of relationships in which one party has nothing new to say. The best way to overcome these problems is to make relationships with those outside a part of the fabric of everyday life in the prison. When contact is frequent, single visits or attempts to contact others are less likely to carry so much weight. Frequent interactions with the outside world may also allow prisoners to retain some of their roles (of partner, parent and friend) on the outside, which in turn can provide their time in prison with much needed texture. The new Chief Executive of the Scottish Prison Service called for phones in cells in front of the Scottish Government's Justice Committee in January 2013 (Dinwoodie, 2013). If such phones could take incoming calls, this would allow for more normal contact between a prisoner and those outside. For example, if they can phone whenever they want, children, partners and friends can call on the prisoner for emotional (if not practical) support during difficult times. Unfortunately, after a largely negative public reaction to this proposal, it was ruled out by the Cabinet Secretary for Justice, Kenny MacAskill (Herald Scotland, 27 February 2013). If phones in cells really are too radical a suggestion for these times, other ways should be found to maintain relationships as part of the day-to-day routine. Soon after the rejection of the phones in cells, the Justice Committee suggested that prisoners get access to the internet for educational purposes (Justice Committee, 2013). Perhaps in time, such access can also be used to stay connected to people, rather than just events and knowledge, in the outside world.

Individual support

One of the topics on which most of the anger and frustration was expressed in the interviews was rehabilitation. As noted in Chapter 3, a common

view among the men was that they needed greater individual attention and support to be able to move away from offending upon release.
Ideally, resources would be made available to offer prisoners counselling
and other personalised interventions (see also Burnett, 2004). However,
current developments in one Scottish prison suggest that it might be
possible to create a more individualised experience, without necessarily
a great increase in investment, as a first step. HMP Greenock is rolling
out a one-to-one model that has already been implemented amongst its
female population. Each prisoner will have an allocated prison officer
who accompanies them throughout their sentence. Rather than the
prison intake process, assessments and support being carried out by
different members of staff, all these tasks will be completed by the same
officer, allowing this officer to be better aware of the prisoner's circumstances and creating the time, space and consistency for more meaningful relationships to develop. This approach is complemented by the
creation of two Throughcare Support Officers, who will work with prisoners to tackle reintegration issues during their time in prison and for up
to twelve weeks after their release. In time, this throughcare support will
hopefully also be undertaken by personal officers, so that the relationship developed during the prisoners' time inside can facilitate their motivation to seek support and overcome problems upon release (Kerr 2013,
personal communication). By extending the role of personal officers in
this way, HMP Greenock will be moving in the opposite direction from
Whitemoor, where the personal officer role was diminished (Liebling
and Arnold, 2012, p. 422). This might to some extent address the need
for more individual attention and input for prisoners. Prison officers will
have to have an array of possible activities, courses and interventions at
their disposal, so that the support package offered to the prisoner can
also be personalised. If, instead, all the officer can do is refer prisoners to
the same old semi-compulsory cognitive behavioural programmes, then
not much will be gained. However, if personal officers are able to get to
know prisoners well enough so that any intervention is offered at the
right time, when there is motivation to change, and can keep prisoners
connected to their life outside, then prisoners might not be so ready to
survive their sentence by turning inwards. Ensuring that prisoners have
individual input and interest from staff might be one step towards delivering a prison regime that succeeds in its aim of rehabilitation.

Judicial rehabilitation

A final important finding of this book for policy and practice was
the way in which the lack of opportunities to develop new identities

stalled the progressive stories of transformation and reform for the men on licence. With the main desired identity one of being gainfully employed, which was made difficult by their criminal record, this unintended consequence of imprisonment can be tackled through a change in policy. Maruna and McNeill have recently focused on the concept of judicial rehabilitation (Maruna, 2011a, b; McNeill, 2012, 2013), which Maruna argues should form part of a redemption ritual. Criminal records should be expunged or a certificate of rehabilitation issued so that the person is re-accepted into the community, and given the same chances as other citizens to achieve their goals and contribute to society at large (Maruna, 2011a, b). Research has shown that those convicted of offences before the age of 20 are little more likely to commit further offences after the age of 30 than those without any convictions (Soothill and Francis, 2009). Others have found that those who were first arrested at 20 were actually *less* likely to reoffend after five crime-free years than the general population (Blumstein and Nakamura, 2009). Of course, most of the participants in this research had substantial criminal histories, rather than a single arrest, but once crime free, their statistical chances of reconviction are likely to be similar, especially as increasing age reduces the likelihood of subsequent offending (ibid.). In any case, there is no reason why crimes punished by long-term prison sentences should be disclosed forever. In fact, Maruna (2011a) argues that convictions should expire or be neutralised by a certificate of rehabilitation *before* desistance is a certainty, in order to encourage rehabilitation, rather than only to reward it after it has become more or less certain. This makes the end of the licence period a suitable point in time for judicial rehabilitation for those serving the longest sentences. Their desistance during the licence period is something that is already noted by criminal justice authorities; if any serious offending had come to light, they would have been returned to prison. By the end of this period, anyone with a sentence of over nine years will have already spent at least three years on licence, more or less crime-free. Maruna has also written of the end of licence as a suitable time for judicial rehabilitation:

> The conclusion of a probationary period after prison, for instance, might logically involve a return to the courtroom for the ritualised certification of a 'clean bill of health' after the sentence's completion. All debts would be officially paid in full and the individual would be allowed to move on with the rest of his or her life with no further collateral consequences or restrictions. (Maruna, 2011a, pp. 111–112)

For those serving shorter sentences, the redemption ritual might need to include a promise of future judicial rehabilitation, for example after three years in the community.

In other jurisdictions, the impact of the criminal record is already far more restricted than in the UK. In France sentences longer than two years are recorded for three to ten years afterwards (Herzog-Evans, 2011b), in the Netherlands for four years (Boone, 2011) and in Germany for five years (Morgenstern, 2011). Significantly, people are much less likely to be asked to disclose their convictions when they apply for a position. In France, those with a criminal record are under no obligation to disclose this if they are not asked by their prospective employer, and employers tend to ask only if the person is to be employed in a position of trust (Herzog-Evans, 2011b). In Germany, a person is not obliged to reveal their criminal record unless they are applying for a role in which personal integrity is indispensable, and even then they only need to reveal relevant convictions (for example, traffic offences for lorry drivers) (Morgenstern, 2011). If a shorter time-frame for judicial rehabilitation, as proposed above, was combined with restricting the types of jobs for which disclosure is necessary, then people leaving prison would have some hope of finding a job with limited responsibility initially, followed by potentially more satisfying employment at the end of their licence period or soon thereafter. In this way, they would follow a destigmatising employment trajectory, like the one described by Goffman in his work on stigma (1990). By allowing them to 'make normal' before potentially 'making good', any progressive narratives told by ex-prisoners could continue their upward trajectory.

Appendix I: Narrative Vignettes

Start of sentence

Chris

Chris was in his early forties and an easy talker. He had no teeth, but told me he had been handsome in the past and was looking forward to getting new dentures. Things had gone well for him when he was young: he had worked as a plumber for the council, had opened his own clothing store and dated models. His downfall began when his dad died and Chris was arrested with a few XTC tablets, just after the first deaths attributed to XTC occurred in the UK. He received an 18-month sentence and while imprisoned started using heroin when mandatory drug testing came in, making using cannabis to relieve boredom and his grief over his father's death difficult. He left prison addicted. Several more prison sentences followed for shoplifting and the possession of class A drugs. The sentence he was serving was imposed for couriering a large amount of drugs in order to pay off a debt to his dealer. Chris was one of the few interviewees critical of the use of imprisonment. In cases like his own, he felt it should be the big drug dealers in prison, not 'the little guys' like himself. He also blamed the accumulation of sentences in his life for greatly exacerbating his problems. In general, he noted that those who are in prison tend to be uneducated and that there should be better ways to help them. Nevertheless, he ascribed a positive meaning to his current sentence, seeing it as a benign intervention from above.

> So in the back of my mind this jail was my sort of eehm/ was an eehm an escape for me, really, to actually get clean and that ... This has been thrown at me at this time in my life yeah, because of my age and to get eehm/ to start a fresh start, that's what I think [laughs] ... that's what the, whoever the Almighty is, was thinking. That it's time.

End of sentence

Alex

Alex was in his late thirties, very well-spoken and from an affluent background. He attributed his offending to a need for excitement combined with a high tolerance for risk. After serving one long-term sentence in his twenties for robbery he had become involved in drug dealing and the intimidation of other drug dealers. He maintained his innocence of his index offence (attempted murder) throughout the interview, but admitted to other crimes of which he had not been convicted, so felt that his sentence was 'fair enough' even though he was appealing it. With his parents on another continent and not much else keeping him in the UK, Alex planned to use money from earlier property investments plus the compensation he expected to receive when his appeal was successful to move abroad and set up a legitimate business after the end of his licence. He saw imprisonment as an occupational hazard, but one that did make crime less attractive. He experienced prison as aversive, especially the deprivation of variety and stimulation it entailed. The overall meaning of his sentences was a large negative on the balance sheet of his life.

> The weighting's all wrong. I mean, I'm obviously not smart or skilful enough that (.) it's disproportionate. Overall, the balance is wrong. IT'S not, it's not been a profitable or prosperous, if I take the whole, all criminality on my part as a whole, it's NOT been a profitable or prosperous enterprise. Because what we're talking about here is four years of kind of, you know, very eehm, accentuated living, for twelve years in prison.

Colin

Colin was in his early thirties, but seemed much younger. He tended not to tell extended stories so much as listing events (like his sentences). He came from a chaotic family and had a child, but did not have any contact with his ex-partner. His past offences included driving cars without a licence, selling stolen car parts and shoplifting and he had served several short prison sentences, enough for him to have lost track of what sentence followed what offence. He started drug dealing to fund his own drug use and was given his first long-term sentence for dealing in Class A drugs. He saw his prison sentence as necessary for his transformation.

> Well, I am really glad I got it now, eh? Well, I managed to get off all the drugs and that. I have touched nothing since I came into this jail. I have been stable- I am on methadone, eh, I have been stable on that for three years now, and that is the first time I have been clean, so it has really done, really done me good this sentence, eh?

Dan

In his 60s, Dan was one of the oldest prisoners I interviewed. He had been convicted of murder in his early 20s for killing someone in a pub fight and had served twelve years on a life sentence back then. His wife had stuck by him, and afterwards they had built up a good life with their children. Dan's more recent downfall started when he and his wife separated. He started drinking and ended up stabbing a female friend without any provocation, for which he was given a long-term prison sentence. More recently, he had stabbed a teenager who was part of a group of people drinking at Dan's house, again without provocation. Dan struggled to make sense of these offences himself. He found this sentence much harder to bear than his previous ones, because he missed his wife, who had died in the interim. Even after they had separated, she had remained an important source of support for him during his previous sentence. He used the interview as a eulogy to her loyalty, contrasting this with his own stupidity. His daughters, from whom he was estranged, were only described with anger. Indeed, his main motivation for trying to rebuild his life was showing them he did not need them. The overarching meaning of his prison sentence was a time-out that allowed him to think and re-group. However, he was not sure this process would lead to desistance, as he did not understand his offending himself and was not certain he could control it.

> I've had time to think in here. I've had a lot of time on my hands. More so this sentence than any other sentence because I'm on my own. On my previous, my wife was always there, she always stood by me, a solid address to go to, etcetera, and all of that. Now I've had to rethink my whole life again, I'm starting from (.) as I say, I'm starting from scratch.

Devan

Devan was in his early twenties and imprisoned for his first offence: the possession of a large amount of drugs. He described a happy upbringing and had still been living at home with his mother and younger brothers when his girlfriend got pregnant. Due to the pressure he felt to set up a home and 'make the family work', he dropped out of college and rented a flat. Unable to find a job and needing to pay back a loan he had taken out in order to tide himself over, he agreed to courier drugs by train. Because he saw himself as having been pushed by circumstances, Devan took little responsibility for his crime, unlike most of the men. He was also almost alone in opposing his sentence throughout the interview. Devan was confident that he would be able to desist upon release, with the support of his family, and good prospects of returning to a job he held between arrest and conviction. The overall meaning of his sentence in his narrative was a dislocation into a gritty drama, which so far had only been familiar from TV, but one in which he claimed the starring role.

> So in the back of my head I'm thinking to myself, all these prison programmes that I've seen before and all the kinds of things I have heard about this happens in jails and all of that, I'm thinking to myself 'first things first, I'm going to let this guy know it ain't about that kind of thing'. So, [laughs] I had to make sure that he knew that I'm not that way inclined and make sure that he knew that if he tries something like that it's gonna kick off, because there is no way that I'm allowing them kind of things to happen.... We got to sit down and talking and he had some cigarettes on him, or tobacco or whatever, and I'm just thinking to myself 'tobacco? I see old men smoking that, there's no way I could be smoking that'. I'm thinking to myself 'what have I got myself into?'

Doug

Doug was an equable man in his late twenties. He had previously received short-term sentences for breach of the peace and resisting arrest, but was serving a four years sentence at the time of the interview. Suspecting that a man was following the daughter of friends he was staying with, Doug had repeatedly stabbed him. Doug had always had a difficult relationship with his family, who broke off all contact with him when he received his sentence. Because of this, he relied more on relationships with his friends and their families, but discouraged their visits, as it was a long journey for them and it was difficult to find things to talk about. Before his sentence Doug was working on fishing boats and he was quite confident that he would be able to return to this after his release. On the other hand he was very worried about his accommodation status as he had previously been evicted from council housing. Doug was glad that his time in prison was passing quickly, but at the same time saw this passing of time as its main meaning: a tax on the best years of his life.

> the way I seen my sentence is, the time goes by so quick in here, that (.) it goes by quick but you age quick and you realise that life is just going by and you're stuck in here, so your years are getting took right off you.

Gordon

Gordon was young, in his early twenties, and maintained that he had not committed the offence for which he was imprisoned. There had been a big gang fight, from which his older brother had gone on to stab someone, and Gordon had been convicted as his co-offender, even though Gordon said he had left by that point. Despite his protestation of innocence and this being his first imprisonment, Gordon was very positive about his sentence. He felt that he would have committed a serious crime sooner or later, and that this sentence had prevented him from doing so. More importantly, because he had engaged with all the activities on offer, he felt he would be in a better position upon his release to resist the temptation of crime. Gordon was close to his mother, his main source of support. He had absconded from the open estate when he felt he was starting to become addicted to heroin there. While on the run, he had met his new girlfriend, whom he described as a 'straight peg' and therefore as a positive influence. Overall, prison's meaning to Gordon was an opportunity to change himself for the better.

> Makes me, makes me in a good way feel now, looking back, that maybe the best thing was that I have done this sentence, now my eyes are open and I come out with a different attitude and a different aspect and look at things different, you know? And really, to go from 18 and now I'm going out, 24, I'm going about with my eyes open, I'm not going to be running about like a daft wee boy, out in the street drinking, stealing cars. I'm planning to get out, get a house and settle down with my girlfriend.

Graham

Graham was in his early thirties and seemed uncomfortable with the interview process. He often would give very short answers and then look away. Since he was 17 he had spent most of his time in prison, but on short-term sentences for offences such as car thefts and assaults. He was serving four years for punching a man who had subsequently died. Before this offence Graham had been homeless, sleeping on the sofas of friends and in hostels and he felt his life had been in a downward spiral from which prison had saved him. He had a daughter with his fiancée, and being away from them was the most painful aspect of his imprisonment for him. However, his relationship had been jeopardised when Graham had asked his fiancée to supply drugs to him in prison, for which offence she had received community service. She and their child were living with her parents, who would not let Graham in the house, so while he hoped he would be able to mend his relationship upon his release, he was not confident. Graham did not ascribe a clear meaning to his prison sentence. On the one hand he felt it had changed his attitude, but on the other he felt he had not been rehabilitated and was ambivalent about his future offending.

> I don't know, it has made me look at things a lot, a lot clearer (.). Maybe had a good look at my life and do I want to keep on using drugs... All that's done is took me away from my wee girl, took me away from a bond, I've lost my wee girl, I'll have to try to get her back. ... I hope to get my life sorted, but they just keep on putting me in hos/ it's not going to work. Something will happen, I'll do something again, y'know.

Ian

Ian was a slight man in his early thirties, who looked older than his age. He very briefly referred to being severely physically abused in childhood during the interview. He received his first prison sentence aged 15 and had spent little time outside of prison since then. Most of his convictions had been for assaults, robberies and attempted murders and he seemed to relish the retelling of some of the more violent incidents. After his last sentence he had managed to stay out of prison for two and a half years, two of which on licence. He felt that the support and expectations upon him while he was on licence had been helpful in curbing his offending. During this time he had entered his first relationship with a woman and had a child with her. Problems between them started soon after the baby was born, and just a few weeks after the birth Ian was arrested for robbery. Ian said he had had to resort to crime in order to provide for his child. He received a seven-year sentence with a three-year extended licence. Ian found this sentence much more painful than his previous ones because he knew the time he was missing with his son would never come back. His relationship with his partner had also broken down. Ian said that this sentence he had tried to engage with the resources available in the prison to achieve some kind of rehabilitation, but so many obstacles were put in his way that he had disengaged to the point where he refused to take drug tests, did not apply for parole and refused to work. Despite its painfulness, he also saw his sentence as a 'break' and imprisonment as normal. Consequently, he was ambivalent about his release.

I know it's cruel to say something like that but I'm, this is the things I'm thinking about, because I'm that used to being in here myself, no pressure, with no pressure, no hassle, and then going out with a wean screaming all the time. You know what I'm talking about, it's just (.).

James

James was in his late thirties and was serving his second long-term sentence. He has served a few short-term sentences in the past, usually as a consequence of refusing to abide by probation or community service conditions. He was serving just over ten years for two counts of drug possession and taking part in a group assault within the prison. He had cut off contact with his father and sister for the duration of his imprisonment, but was hoping to live with his father upon release. His time in prison had made James reflect on the alternative life he could have lived if he had not 'made the wrong choices', as he put it. He described his life as severely lacking in comparison to this ideal, in that he had no wife, no children, no house and no job prospects. Nevertheless, he told a positive narrative in which his sentence had made him think and changed him for the better.

> [It's made me think about] everything, just (.) life, aye. How I ... wasted it, what could have happened, you ken what I mean, I COULD HAVE had a better life, if I'd just took a different path, so. It's helped me make my mind up what path I'm going to choose when I get out. (.) I've learned from it, a lot. ... A lesson, it has been a lesson to me, a valuable one, definitely.

Peter

Peter was one of the youngest amongst the interviewees, in his early 20s, and from the start of the interview was quite guarded in his answers. He had been in care for most of his childhood while his siblings remained in the family home. Previously Peter had only received short-term sentences for driving offences, despite also dealing drugs. At the time of the interview Peter was imprisoned for ten years for his involvement in a group killing: he and his associates had assaulted someone he had never met before that day but who was known to others in the group. They had left him unconscious and Peter only learned he had died from watching the news on TV. He described feeling awful about what had happened and said that it had been a relief to be arrested. For part of the interview, Peter positioned prison as the best thing that could have happened to him and described how he had learned to be much less confrontational and to avoid fights. However, when his story of transformation through imprisonment became untenable in the interview, he switched to a different perspective, with him the victim of the state's interventions. However, he still supported his current imprisonment as inevitable given the likelihood that he would reoffend.

> I'll keep on doing things [wrong] anyway, ken what I mean, so it's not, that's why I just agree with it. I'm, I'm going to get into trouble again, I probably will get into trouble again, even though I don't want to, I'll probably end up back in prison, so (.) ten years is probably good for me.

On licence

Andy

Andy was in his late twenties and was quite agitated and frustrated from the start of the interview. He had served previous short-term sentences and describes how, before his latest offence, he had tried and failed to get help with his mental health, feeling aggression and paranoia building. He was convicted for stabbing a man who his friend had provoked into a fight. Despite his friend being the aggressor, when it started to look like he was getting hurt Andy got involved. Looking back he saw his response as 'WELL over the top, I mean there was no need for to use a knife, you know what I mean, absolutely no need, I could have easily probably used my hands'. He accepted his prison sentence as fair and said he had benefited greatly from using the gym, which had increased his confidence, and from the discipline in prison. Since his release he no longer felt he needed to carry a knife, but had been involved in at least one further fight. The meaning of imprisonment for him was one of transformation, but being unable to find a job, he felt this progress was threatened, which left him frustrated and upset.

> Obviously I've changed as a person but pfff, I was saying to [my social worker] the last time I was down, 'financially I'm at the worst I've ever been in my whole life', know what I mean. This is me supposed to be at my best as a person and yet I'm at my worst in other areas so (.) so it's horrible man, absolutely horrible.

Jack

Jack was in his early forties, but looked older. He had spent most of his adult life in prison, typically spending only a couple of months in the community between long sentences. He characterised his offences as 'robberies and everything', but was one of the few participants not to go into detail, except to say that he had committed all his offences under the influence of alcohol or drugs. At the time of the interview it had been almost two years since his last release. He credited this change in direction to his own motivation, but also to the support he had received from his social worker and his girlfriend. Despite these positive developments, Jack described life outside as a struggle. He found carrying out routine tasks, such as paying bills or arranging doctor appointments difficult, and felt that his criminal record 'blew' any chance of finding a job 'right out of the water'. For him being imprisoned was a normal state of affairs that he found difficult to move away from.

> It didn't bother me one bit, you know what I mean, going in or whatever, cause it was like a second home to me. I probably spend a lot more time in there than I have out here...and when I get up I've got a job every morning, I go to the gym, go and play pool, go and do whatever, then come night time you're tired for half nine, ten o'clock, out here you can't sleep till two and three in the morning.

Lino

Lino was in his late thirties and presented himself as an optimist who had reformed himself. His most recent sentence had been for carrying a knife, which he felt had been unfair, but he was largely supportive of his earlier sentences, condemning his own offending. He described his younger self as anti-authoritarian, impulsive and thrill seeking. With age he felt he had 'mellowed out', and he avoided any potential trouble by staying home most of the time. He described his family as very supportive and as having helped him to think about the impact of his actions. His daughter telling him that she did not want a dad in prison was a turning point for Lino, motivating him to desist. Lino felt he needed help with his mental health before he could make other progressive steps, such as finding employment. The meaning of his latest sentence for Lino was complex. He was angry he had been imprisoned for carrying a knife, but felt that to cope with and to make sense out of his time in prison, it needed to have positive consequences.

It was after I decided to come off the drugs, (.) then I tried to take somethin' good out of me despising the coppers for what they'd done and hating the fact that I'm in jail for doing nothing, for carrying something in my pocket and I wasn't doing anything negative towards anybody. If I didn't, then I think it would have been much harder for me to deal with the four-year sentence.

Mohammed

Mohammed was in his early thirties, but looked younger. He was open about his past and his heroin addiction and talked easily. He had most recently been convicted of attacking someone who had hurt his younger half-brothers. His previous sentences had been for assault and robbery and drug offences. While imprisoned, Mohammed met his biological father for the first time, along with other relatives from that side of his family. He said of them 'I keep my distance because they'll never change, they're always going to be like that, in and out of prison. And it's not something I want.' Mohammed's younger half-brothers both had gone on to serve prison sentences of their own. He felt responsible for this, because they looked up to him and he felt he had set a bad example. A large part of Mohammed's motivation to stop offending was to avoid becoming like his father. On licence, Mohammed was struggling to find a job and keenly felt the stigma of having a serious criminal record. He was one of the only interviewees to admit to having found imprisonment very painful and difficult, and this was the overarching meaning of his sentence for him. Wanting to avoid further sentences provided him with further motivation to desist.

> But (.) I don't think I would go back. Well, if I went back I don't think [short laugh] I don't think I'd hack it too well. I think I would either try and escape or commit suicide or something, because I wouldn't go back for any length of time, I don't like/ it's (.) I can't imagine it, it scares me thinking about it.

Tony

Tony was in his early fifties, but muscular and looked much younger. He was the only one in his family to have been in any trouble, saying he was 'always a rogue' and had served several long-term and numerous short-term sentences, mostly for assaults and robberies. He saw these sentences as an occupational hazard, but was still upset about a wrongful sentence for rape he had served in the early 1980s. He spent a long time explaining exactly what had happened and how he had come to be framed for it. As he said 'they gave me three year and I hated every day of it, it killed me, it killed me every day'. Since his release, Tony had done well for himself. He had set up his own gardening business and this had been very successful. Tony had been on three foreign holidays that year and had taken on his brother to keep up with demand. He also had not used alcohol or drugs since his release. Despite these successes, Tony saw himself as institutionalised and described how he had resisted being released from his most recent sentence, because he 'didn't want the responsibility'. In the interview, he returned again and again to the comfort and predictability of his life in prison, describing it in terms more suitable to a retreat centre than a criminal punishment. For Tony, this seemed to be what prison had become.

> I was content in my wee (.) in my wee world and I just used to go up, go to the gym, get fed, work about, cleaning offices and that and then early to bed, nine o'clock and up at five the next and it was great, I loved it, sitting in my cell...And I used to just sit there and I could sit there for hours and just look (.) look at the ferns out in the hills, cause they always build these places away out in the wild. And then they started...the meetings in there you've got to start getting ready to go to open conditions, 'I'm not going' I was fed up hearing myself saying it 'I'm not going', 'I'm not going'.

Appendix II: Narrative Methods

Introduction

This Appendix discusses the reasons for choosing a narrative methodology, as well as looking in depth at the form and function of narratives according to two different approaches, both of which informed the
research. Implications for the analysis stage and the claims that can be
made about the standing of its findings are considered. The final section
considers the impact I, as the audience, will have had on the narratives
the men constructed in the interviews.

Rationale for narrative methods

A narrative methodology was chosen because it had several contribu-
tions to make across the project, and was essential in order to answer
individual research questions. A narrative methodology allowed participants to present the meaning life events had for them in their own
terms (Polkinghorne, 2007), letting the audience 'enter the perspective
of the narrator' (Riessman, 2008, p. 9). In addition, narrative analysis
left the stories told intact, rather than fragmenting them and comparing
them to fragments of other interviews (Lieblich, Tuval-Mashiach and
Zilber, 1998). This was essential in order to consider what meanings prisoners ascribed to a long-term sentence and how these and the sentence's
legitimacy were interpreted in relation to their wider life story.

Besides maintaining the integrity of the interviewees' views, Riessman
(2002) has argued that displaying or describing narratives in research
findings often creates empathy for the narrators, more than the use
of fragmented snippets of conversation divorced of their context, and
has the ability to bridge the gap between people from different social
backgrounds or groups. This was invaluable in this research project, as
offenders' views of their sentence have largely been ignored and might
be seen as immaterial by a large proportion of the public and criminal
justice staff. As Maguire (2000) has argued in relation to ethnography,
presenting offenders' accounts provides a reminder that offenders are
people, not just numbers to be managed; something that is in danger
of being forgotten within criminal justice policy. In fact, Feeley and
Simon (1992) have influentially argued that criminal justice practice

no longer focuses on individual offenders and their outcomes, but instead on managing them as an aggregate, and have called this the New Penology (see also Cheliotis, 2006; Crewe, 2009; Robinson, 2008). With the individuality of offenders often ignored in the media, where they are presented as the 'dangerous other', and arguably in criminal justice practice, criminology has also been accused in the past of tending 'to generalise, to stereotype, to reduce, to objectify, and to silence the human beings who fall under its gaze' (Garland, 1992, p. 419), thereby underwriting the notion that offenders are 'alien others' (Garland, 1992, p. 418), fundamentally different from the law-abiding public at large. Long-term prisoners, especially, are 'othered' and presented as 'the worst of the worst'.[1]

Furthermore, narrative analysis made it possible to investigate what type of identity participants presented. This type of analysis was also useful in my research, for example, in Chapter 5, where I examined the difference between the men in prison and those on licence in the extent to which they presented themselves as in control of their own destiny. In this, I have built on work by Riessman (2002), who described how narrators can position themselves as active agents or passive victims, or both in different domains within their stories, and Maruna (2001) who carried out a similar analysis in relation to control over re-offending.

What are narratives?

Different authors locate the origin of narrative research in different times, depending on their discipline. Some refer to the life-stories examined by the Chicago School of Sociology (Chase, 2005), while others go further back to the Russian formalists (Franzosi, 1998) or Freud's case studies (McAdams, 2001). However, there is broad agreement that it was with the 'narrative turn' in the 1980s that interest in narratives really burgeoned in psychology (McAdams, 2001), social science, various other disciplines and as a focal point in popular culture (Riessman, 2008; Stanley and Temple, 2008). As a consequence, narrative approaches have proliferated, often with different conceptions of what narratives are, how they should be analysed and what they can tell us (Stanley and Temple, 2008). At present, narrative research 'remains a relative open intellectual space characterized by diversity but also fragmentation' (Stanley and Temple, 2008, p. 276). There is no unifying theory and, accordingly, little guidance on how to conduct 'proper' narrative research – methods endorsed by one author are often called into question by others (e.g., Atkinson, 1997; Riessman and Quinney, 2005).

An influential definition of narratives formulated by Labov states that narratives are 'one method of recapitulating past experience by matching a verbal sequence of clauses to the sequence of events which (it is inferred) actually occurred' (1972, pp. 359–360). In line with this, Labov insists that it should make sense after each narrative clause to ask 'what happened then?', with this question providing the link to the next part of the narrative (2010). While most authors agree that there has to be *some* logical connection between different parts of a narrative, and many still insist on temporal ordering (Franzosi, 1998), others have argued that this focus on time is a feature of the dominant Western form of storytelling (Pavlenko, 2002). Research with school children from different ethnic backgrounds in North America has shown that narrative clauses can be linked by theme or space as well as time (Michaels and Cazden, 1984; Michaels, 1981). Narratives also do not necessarily refer to a single chain of events that 'really' occurred. Alternative types of narratives have been identified, such as habitual narratives, where ongoing and repeated events are described, and hypothetical narratives about wished for events that never took place (Riessman, 1997). Labov's structural definition of narratives also left out elements that others consider essential. Aristotle recognised that narratives are inevitably built around characters enacting a plot (McQuillan, 2000). There is a further expectation that these characters undertake purposive actions. As McAdams writes:

> in virtually all intelligible stories, humans ... act to accomplish intentions upon a social landscape, generating a sequence of action and reactions extended as a plot in time. (2008, p. 250)

Furthermore, children as young as five already expect stories to have a clear beginning and middle and an ending that resolves the complications and tensions introduced during its telling (McAdams, 2008). Narratives, then, describe events which are linked in some way (in time, by theme or spatially) and are initiated and reacted to by the characters involved. Earlier parts of the narrative explain what follows, while the ending typically rounds off the story by providing a resolution of some sort.

What do narratives achieve?

Labov's (2010) view of narratives as reflecting events that actually happened, has been called into further question in discussions of the purpose of narratives. Writers on qualitative research warn against seeing interviews as 'pipelines' (Holstein and Gubrium, 1997) that transfer information held by the participant on what happened to the researcher. Instead, interviews are sites of meaning construction; the participant is not a passive 'vessel of answers', but

> in the very process of offering up [experiences], constructively adds to, takes away from, and transforms them into artefacts of the occasion. (ibid., p. 145)

Two main interpretations of the way in which narrators shape and use narratives, informed the research reported in this book. The constructivist perspective sees narratives as a situated performance, with its form dependent on the circumstances and the audience (e.g., Labov, 2010; Norrick, 2005; Polanyi, 1985; Riessman, 2008). On the other hand, those who emphasise the importance of narrative identity, hereafter called the identity perspective, see each narrative as part of an ongoing project by the narrator to integrate their different experiences and behaviours into a coherent life story (e.g., Josselson, 1995; Maruna, 2001; McAdams, 2008; Pavlenko, 2002; Singer, 2004).

Emphasising the persuasive purpose of narratives, Riessman defines narratives as connecting events into a sequence that is consequential for later action and for the meanings that the speaker wants listeners to take away from the story (Riessman, 2008, p. 3). Polanyi (1985) similarly argues that narrators generate stories themselves and take responsibility for their relevance. Labov (2010) stresses the importance of what he terms evaluative clauses in the narrative, in which the speaker justifies the relevance of their story to the audience, thereby pre-empting the potential question of 'so what?'. According to these constructivist perspectives, the narrator moulds the narrative in order to communicate a point, but the audience or interviewer also has an active role in the construction of meaning. They shape the narrative first of all through their characteristics as an audience (Presser, 2008). Riessman (2002), drawing on Goffman (1959), describes the construction of narrative as a performance with participants presenting a preferred version of themselves, rather than some 'true' version of themselves or their experience. This aspect of narratives may be especially salient in the case of offenders, who may find it more necessary than others to shape their narratives so that they are not perceived in an overly negative light (Riessman, 2002, p. 701). What version of themselves they see as 'preferred' will depend on the audience. Besides having certain characteristics as an audience, the interviewer asks questions and reacts during the interview, which will have an impact on the narrative told. Norrick (2005) discusses some of the ways in which audiences provide feedback to the narrator about the acceptability and relevance of their story, which include (not) interrupting, body language such as facing the narrator and nodding, making appreciative noises such as 'mmm', and laughter. Such signals will influence the length of the narrative, but also which parts of it will be most developed. In a research setting the narrative, then, is constructed between the interviewer and the interviewee, and a product of the encounter, although influenced by forces and events beyond the interview setting.

The alternative perspective, which emphasises narratives' role in the formation of identity, sees separate narrative occasions as drawing on a life story that the narrator has constructed to make sense of their lives (McAdams, 2008). The life story is seen as a life-long project, which brings together our disparate experiences and roles, explains how one led to another and connects these with our goals and motivations (Habermas and Bluck, 2000). In this way, we come to know who we are and give our lives meaning (McAdams, 2008). This, in turn, influences how we behave, because we tend to act in ways that are in keeping with who we think we are (McAdams, 2001). There even is debate about whether we *interpret* experiences in a narrative form or whether narratives *constitute* reality, because we cannot experience events without narrating them (Presser, 2008). Either way, some strong claims have been made for the importance of life stories. For example, McAdams claims that, along with dispositional traits and characteristic adaptations, the type of narrative a person constructs about their life explains the differences between individuals (2001). This demands considerable constancy from such life stories, suggesting that narratives generally do not vary excessively in different contexts.

However, the two perspectives are not as disparate as they seem and some researchers see narratives as both being essential to identity *and* a situated performance (see Presser, 2008). Both approaches had much to contribute to the research, but in combination. Most people do construct some sort of internal life story, but this might never come to be narrated as a whole, and may be a lot less coherent and all-encompassing than the identity perspective suggests. While older experiences may be given a comprehensive place in this underlying life story, newer events may still be interpreted in a more fluid way. Josselson (1995) found, when interviewing women several times over 20 years, that elements that were important in a story at one point disappeared from view later, only to sometimes re-emerge as significant as the interviewees' view of themselves and their life story changed. Narratives are revised as the future becomes our present and fails to unfold exactly as we imagined it when we told our earlier stories. I would argue that recent events are not only more sensitive to changed interpretations on the basis of further experience, but also to the impact of the audience, their questions, and so on. This was borne out by the interviews. One participant, Peter, switched from one kind of account of his sentence to a completely contradictory one because he could not maintain the coherence of the former (see Chapter 4). Also, the men who were coming to the end of their sentence had more freedom to project possible futures upon release than those on licence, for whom the meaning of their sentence was more determined by their current circumstances (see Chapter 5).

In addition, when given different prompts by their audience, narrators may tell stories that highlight different aspects of their identity, which could to some extent be contradictory. For example, a long-term prisoner might portray himself as a 'hard man', who does not care about others' feelings, to one kind of audience, while he might present himself as a caring father to another. However, he might still draw on his sense of who he is and therefore his life story, or at least on identities he feels he can convincingly claim. Narrating a story can be as much a testing out of an identity as the presentation of a settled identity based on a life narrative. Narrative identity scholars who hold that life stories are constructed and sustained in social interaction with others (Gergen and Gergen, 1997) would agree. Pasupathi and Rich (2005) found that if a story was told to a distracted audience, the narrators felt their behaviour in the story was less typical of them afterwards, because they felt the identity they had presented was rejected. They claim that, thereby, social feedback feeds into the life story. This is not necessarily the case in an interview setting, where the narrator does not know the audience well and most likely will not encounter them again. Not being known also gives the narrator the opportunity to tell stories that are less in keeping with their internal life story, if they so choose, and to claim new identities for themselves which they may not have drawn upon before.

Finally, people may vary greatly in the extent to which they construct a coherent life story for themselves. While parts of lives are probably given a definite meaning by most people (an unhappy childhood, for example), some people may have had less opportunity and inclination to reflect on their lives and integrate its different parts than others. With offenders often compared to teenagers in terms of impulsivity, risk taking and being easily influenced (Fabiano, Robinson and

Porporino, 1991; Moffitt, 1993; Walters, 1990), and many living lives that are characterised as 'chaotic' (Social Exclusion Unit, 2002), it seems reasonable to suppose that they especially might not have a fully integrated life story underlying their narratives. Indeed, Vaughan (2007) has argued that some offenders may be what Archer calls 'fractured reflexives'; because they lead such hand-to-mouth existences, their 'capacity to hold an internal conversation with themselves in relation to their circumstances, which has any efficacy' (Archer, 2003, cited in Vaughan, 2007, p. 397) is eroded. On the other hand, long-term sentences might provide offenders with the reflective space and time they need to (re) consider their lives. The variability in the coherence of life stories is acknowledged in the literature on narrative identities, with stories of greater complexity and coherence seen as indications of greater maturity of the narrator (McAdams, 2008).

Integrating these perspectives means that in analysing the interviews, the men's narratives were treated as a performance, influenced by its audience, context and setting, but a performance that drew to varying degrees on an underlying inner-self story constructed by the narrator to make sense of their lives. In the paragraphs above I have identified some factors that influence the extent to which the narrated content will draw on a coherent life story, including the narrator, when the narrated events took place and the familiarity of the audience, but there will be many others.

Other influences on narratives

While the above discussion focuses on the influence of the immediate research setting and the narrator's sense of self, there is broad agreement that narratives are also influenced by other forces. Silverman (2001) points out that underlying any story are 'widespread cultural assumptions' (ibid., p. 96), which put constraints on what can be told. While stories told by North Americans, for example, tend to focus on significant events in the narrator's life and their actions and emotions, those told by Chinese narrators tend to be less self-focused, centre around historical or social events and emphasise relationships (Wang and Conway, 2004). Even within one culture, dominant discourses change over time: Pavlenko (2002) points out that in the early 20th century in the US narratives of immigrants tended to draw on the 'rags-to-riches' theme, whereas in the 60s and 70s, when ethnicity and race were becoming more salient in the wider culture, stories were much more likely to centre around issues of race identity and oppression.

What can be told is also influenced by institutional and group discourses. Miller and Glassner (1997) distinguish between cultural and collective stories, which participants draw on, but can also resist, in an interview. Cultural stories, as the name suggests, are those prevalent in the wider culture (in relation to offenders, for example, that crime should be punished). Collective stories are those that are subscribed to by the group(s) of which the participant is a member (for example, that the best way to get through a prison sentence is 'to get your head down'). Cultural beliefs and those held in the group may overlap, but collective understandings can also oppose cultural beliefs, for example, where the group discourse among prisoners derided cognitive behavioural programmes as a cynical box-ticking exercise.

Narratives are further influenced by the narrator's position within their society. If they belong to a marginalised minority, their story may be less 'tellable', because it is in opposition to the dominant discourses favoured by the powerful. In the case of prisoners, for example, McKendy (2006) found that there were gaps and inconsistencies in their accounts of their offence, because their lived experience of deprivation did not match the officially approved discourse of taking responsibility for one's actions. Again, prisoners and those on licence may be particularly vulnerable to the suppression of their own version of events in favour of the version they feel is expected, as resisting the desired version can have an immediate and serious impact on their lives (such as not being given parole, a negative assessment by a supervising officer and so on). Interestingly, while the prisoners I spoke to seemed pretty open about their illegitimate activities within the prison, those on licence seemed much more wary of the consequences of what they might disclose.

Finally, there are issues of memory and limits on human communication. Polkinghorne (2007) points out that narratives are limited by what participants are willing and able to put into words and what they can remember. It is especially difficult for people to remember their attitudes and beliefs (rather than events) over long periods (Ruspini, 2000). Narratives do not uncover what people thought at the time of the events they are describing, but their current views of their past states (Hindley, 1979).

Narrative analysis

The perspectives on narratives outlined above all informed the analysis of the accounts obtained. Prisoners' stories were not taken at face value but were examined for the impact of the audience, social context, and group and cultural discourses. Participants' motives for telling their particular story were also examined and contradictions explored. On Lieblich et al.'s (1998) classification of research, the analysis carried out was both categorical and holistic: findings arose from comparisons between interviews as well as from comparing extracts of an interview with other parts of the same interview, and trying to integrate the whole. While the emphasis was on content analysis, form was also considered, especially whether interviewees talked about a topic at length and without prompting.

What can the research tell us?

While there is broad agreement that narratives are shaped by aspects of both the immediate and the wider context in which they are told, the construction of meaning in an interview is not completely independent of the participant's life. Glassner and Loughlin (1987) recognise that our thoughts and what we express are derived from our experiences. They argue that it is not necessary to embrace either the idea that interviews produce uncomplicated insights into people's lives, or the opposite extreme, that all meaning in interviews is constructed with no relevance beyond the immediate context. Lieblich, Tuval-Mashiach and Zilber (1998) similarly write:

> We do not advocate total relativism that treats all narratives as texts of fiction. On the other hand, we do not take narratives at face value, as complete and accurate representations of reality. We believe that stories are usually constructed around a core of facts or life events, yet allow a wide periphery for freedom of individuality and creativity in selection, addition to, emphasis on, and interpretation of these 'remembered facts'. (p. 8)

Whereas the above quote allows for individual creativity, it does not mention the many local and cultural influences on narratives. However, it is precisely the opportunity to investigate *why* offenders narrate their sentence and locate them within their lives the way they do that made a narrative methodology ideal for this research.

Given the nature of narrative research, which typically involves only a small number of participants, the aim of the research was not to generalise from the interviews conducted to make claims about what 'all long-term prisoners' or a certain proportion of this group think. In fact, because participant selection was not random, any such generalisations to parent populations are impossible, even if the sample size had been many times larger (Ritchie, Lewis and Elam, 2003). The aim was instead to begin to describe the contours of possibility in long-term prisoners' accounts of their sentences, or the repertoire of narratives that can be told (Silverman, 2001).

Impact of audience

Given my view of narrative interviews as at least partly constructed in the encounter between researcher, interviewee and context, it is important to address the impact I might have had on the narratives produced. Yet, just as each of the men responded in their own individual way to their imprisonment, so they will each have responded differently to me and I will not have been exactly the same during each encounter. For example, my notes on an interview conducted late in the afternoon, the third of the day, when I was four months pregnant read 'I was too tired by this point to effectively steer the interview', while at another time I noted 'I should use longer silences, especially in the part of the interview on legitimacy and purpose to see if I can't get people to reflect more'. Obviously I was a much more active audience in some interviews than in others. Despite this variability in the way I will have influenced the narratives produced, the below is an attempt to assess how I may have affected the findings.

As a female PhD researcher, coming from a comfortable, if foreign and therefore less classifiable, background, there was considerable social distance between the participants and me. This has often been seen as problematic, as there may be a tendency to see those who belong to a different social group as more constrained by their circumstances (which loom large because of their unfamiliarity) than they really are and because their responses, including jargon and gestures, are less easily understood (Bourdieu, 1999). Social proximity also makes it easier to know what questions to ask, and respondents may be hesitant to divulge information to people perceived as a member of an oppressive group (Miller and Glassner, 1997). While I could not alter the fact that I was a PhD student, and therefore lived in a different social world with different expectations of life than my participants, I had a fair understanding of prison jargon, having interviewed many short-term (ex)prisoners previously. My understanding was not perfect, however, as the following surreal exchange illustrates:

> DEVAN: And one day, now, he was picking the sky and when he was picking the sky/
> M: /Yeah, what does that mean?

DEVAN: Nah, sorry, it's just me. Aahm, he was picking the sky and when he was picking the sky.

M: But was does that mean?

DEVAN: Hah? No, nothing, nothing, [both laugh] no, nothing, nothing, nothing. He was genuinely picking the sky, because you get to choose the sky.

M: OKAY, Sky TV channel. I thought you were making a reference to some weird drug use.

Despite the problems involved in social distance, not being a member of the same social group can also have advantages. Participants have the opportunity to feel like an 'expert' on their experience and to 'teach' someone who occupies a more powerful position (Miller and Glassner, 1997). Some of the interviewees clearly relished the occasions where they had a chance to educate me. For example, my notes on my interview with Ian record:

> At times, though, very kind smile, despite all the violence he told me about... Reacted well to me not understanding what he was saying at times, this was often when he smiled. I wish I could have recorded how his face changed then.

In addition, with increasing social distance, less common understanding is assumed, which means that participants may elaborate more on ideas that are taken for granted within the group (Miller and Glassner, 1997). Because the interviewer lacks a common understanding, they are also more likely to ask participants to expand on statements that someone within the group would have understood. Bourdieu (1999), who trained people with close social proximity to his informants to carry out interviews, found that much of the resulting data was uninteresting. He comments:

> One of the major reasons for these failures undoubtedly lies in the perfect match between interviewer and respondent, which lets respondents say everything... except what goes without saying. (1999, p. 612)

The interviewees acted very differently in relation to social distance. Some took great pains to explain what they said. Neil took the most responsibility for rendering his account intelligible, even apologising for his use of language.

Well, I've just had my parole review there, I got a KB, which, sorry, is a slang for knocked back. (Neil)

Here, my foreign nationality seemed to play as much a role as the social distance between us, with common Scottish terms also explained for my benefit.

I used to take my boys there, just wee things like that, little things like that, you sort of miss. (Neil)

Others seemed much less aware or worried that I might not understand them. But when I asked for clarification, this often did produce a more elaborate explanation of the topic at hand.

GRAHAM: There's just, I'm not interested in other people in the jail, you know, I'm doing my own sentence, I'm not wanting to do anybody else's, you know what I mean?

M: Somebody else said that, so what does that mean, doing somebody else's sentence?

GRAHAM: Doing their, going into their wee cliques, if something happens, you're going to have to back them up. No matter, if anything goes down, y'know, you're going to have to do damage to somebody, or somebody is going to do damage to you. That's how it's in the wee cliques, I'd rather keep myself to myself, y'know?

Bourdieu (1999) writes that any research encounter will fit somewhere between the two extremes of perfect social proximity, where nothing will be questioned, and total distance, where a relationship of trust and understanding cannot be established. With my position somewhere in between, it seemed that at least some of the men trusted me enough to speak about themselves and their activities openly.

One aspect of my identity which is likely to have impacted on the way the men spoke is that I am not myself involved in offending. This may have highlighted to the men the need to tell a story of reform or to appeal to a non-offender status in their narratives (Presser, 2010, p. 51), and indeed, very few told me accounts in which they condoned their own offending. For example, Andy said in relation to his conduct in court:

I pled not guilty...I went up to the dock and I lied an everythin', honestly it's horrible.

To another audience, for example a fellow ex-prisoner, he might not have condemned his behaviour in court. There were many such instances where the men distanced themselves from their own behaviour, very possibly in part for my benefit. However, as Presser (2010) has pointed out, any narrative has an audience that shapes what is told. So, while I will have had an impact on what was said, this does not discredit the interview, but does make it important to examine what I brought to the encounter.

A further aspect of my identity which cannot fail to have had an impact, albeit a different one in different interviews, was the fact that I was a woman interviewing men. This seemed to make some of the interviewees protective, especially those who were older, which was expressed in taking responsibility for the intelligibility of what they were saying, as outlined above, and, less tangibly, in the way they spoke to me. Crewe (2006) and Liebling (1999) have noted that male prisoners are more likely to disclose emotions to women than men. Some of our interviews did contain emotional moments, although not one of the men let it go so far that I had to stop the interview process in order to provide appropriate support. Ultimately they all took responsibility for managing their emotions. In other interviews, the male–female dynamic meant that there was a definite tension resembling that of a flirtation or start of a relationship. This dynamic has also been noted by Crowley (2007) and Ezzy (2010), who both describe how they were invited out by interview participants. However, neither author took any responsibility for this outcome or examined why this might have happened; they only record that they 'politely declined' these invitations. Others have highlighted, however, that as researchers we demand high levels of intimacy from qualitative interviews. The ones that feel the most intimate, because the interviewee is genuinely reflecting on their life and motives (the interview as self-observation (Enosh and Buchbinder, 2005)) and reveals much of themselves, are often also the ones that feel the most 'successful' (Birch and Miller, 2000). I would argue that in this sense the best interviews can simulate the intense conversations that often happen at the start of a romantic relationship, which might lead to some confusion for both parties. The interviewer displays levels of interest in the interviewee that would not be acceptable in normal social situations, asks highly personal questions and generally reacts positively to whatever the interviewee chooses to disclose. Cohen and Taylor wrote that, while they were holding classes in a high security wing that evolved into a research encounter, 'for long periods of time we have probably talked more intimately to these men than to any other people we know' (Cohen and Taylor, 1972, p. 33). While in my research most of the self-disclosure was on the part of the interviewees, in some of the interviews the conversation also led to a feeling of intimacy. While this *might* have put more pressure on both interviewer and interviewee to present a more attractive self, instead it seems to have led to a virtuous cycle of further openness. For example, my notes on one of the interviews records:

> Before the start of the interview, he said he was going to Amsterdam with some friends, but in the interview he admitted to having very few friends and being lonely. After the interview the trip to Amsterdam sounded a lot more doubtful. Example of how rapport leads to more self-disclosure.

While this interviewee's social life was only marginally relevant to my research, his openness in admitting to being lonely, not an easy thing to admit to at the best of times, does illustrate how the interview setting had become one in which it was safe to make such disclosures. Although no 'inappropriate' proposals were made at the end of any of my interviews, one or two were the most intense conversations in my life at the time. For me, these interviews required some time for emotional decompression afterwards, and they might have had the same effect on the interviewees, although I have no way of knowing.

Ezzy (2010) argues that it is important to reflect on the emotions one feels about a research topic or situation before the actual interviews. My stance on imprisonment was fairly clear before I started interviewing. As an undergraduate I had written my philosophy dissertation on 'The Justification of Imprisonment' and concluded that imprisonment can only be justified (as exclusion) when offences are so grave that they make it impossible to live in the community with the offender. Having interviewed many short-term prisoners for previous research projects, including one using a longitudinal design, I had also seen the adverse impact of imprisonment on their lives. But because long-term sentences are usually positioned as less unfair than short sentences (Scottish Government, 2007; Scottish Prisons Commission, 2008), and as being only imposed in serious cases, I was expecting to interview people who had committed crimes sufficiently serious to at least warrant imprisonment in my eyes, if not necessarily a long-term sentence. In the end, this was often not the case: some of those I interviewed were imprisoned for couriering drugs for others, throwing one punch at a man who subsequently died, being involved in street fights and causing death by dangerous driving. My view that these offences should not be responded to with imprisonment influenced the way I felt in these interviews and often meant with those at the end of their sentence that my view of their sentence as too harsh and unfair given the circumstances was in conflict with their need to accept their sentence in order to cope. At times I was perhaps too critical for them to freely share their views (see my exchange with James in Chapter 4). However, through reflection and thorough analysis, I feel that my view of their sentence has not overshadowed the interviewees' views, although my critical stance did motivate me to look for explanations for their relatively accepting accounts, something that may not have happened had I been more pro-imprisonment.

Conclusion

The choice of a mainly narrative methodology was informed by the abductive nature of the research question and the lack of previous coherent literature on prisoners' views of their sentence. Narrative analysis was also beneficial in that it encouraged consideration of the whole interview, rather than separated snippets, allowing for the investigation of contradictions and tensions. In this Appendix, I have outlined my understanding of narratives and their function. I have attempted to reconcile approaches that see the telling of narratives as a situated performance with those that emphasise the connection between the told narrative and the life narrative that underlies our identities. As a consequence, the men's narratives are seen as influenced by me as their audience, our interaction, the context of the interview and wider group and cultural discourses, but also as drawing on their internal life story, constructed to make sense of their lives. As the audience for each interview, I will have had a different impact in each encounter, but my identity meant that some of the men felt the need to explain their world, defend their sentence and condemn their offences.

Notes

1   Introduction

1. http://www.poverty.org.uk/e14/index.shtml, accessed 6 March 2014.
2. http://www.sns.gov.uk/, accessed 21 March 2014.

3   Purposes Perceived in the Sentence

1. Actually, Robert had been convicted of offences when he was much younger but had not been in trouble for 40 years before his current imprisonment.
2. The prisoners who had only just started their sentence tended not to mention deterrence as a purpose of imprisonment at all – perhaps because they were not thinking as much about their life after prison and the possibility of reoffending.

4   Legitimacy and the Impact of the Prison Environment

1. Crewe (2009) also repeatedly quotes prisoners as saying they want to 'keep their heads down' (see, for example, pp. 183 and 190), but in relation to pursuing a quiet life within the prison. Burnett and Maruna (2006) quote a prisoner using the same phrase, but in relation to blending in within the prison. It is clear that such phrases can have different meanings, or even carry multiple meanings in one utterance, within the prison context.
2. As noted previously, he separates any fit of people's personal morality with the law from legitimacy, treating the former as a separate concept; another driver for compliance with the law (Tyler, 1990). However, some very recent work on procedural justice and legitimacy has argued that moral alignment, the sense that authorities act 'according to a shared moral purpose with citizens', is important (Jackson et al., 2012, p. 1051), thereby echoing Beetham's (1991) insistence on the justifiability in terms of shared beliefs discussed below.
3. These are not easily assessed because the Scottish criminal justice system is largely based on common law, rather than statute, which means that the rules it follows are not formally recorded (Hutton, 1999). However, consistency and proportionality are mentioned as aims by both textbooks and government reports (Hutton, 1999; Scottish Government, 2008), while 'individualised' sentencing, where the circumstances of the offence and the offender are considered (Hutton, 1999), as well as criminal history (Nicholson, 1981) is referred to in textbooks.

5   Narrative Demands and Desistance

1. Another way to frame the prison sentence in a positive light was to say that, if not imprisoned, you would be dead (usually from drug use, see Chapter 3).

While three interviewees maintained this was the case, it did not dominate their accounts or seem to have the same power as the transformation through imprisonment narrative discussed here, perhaps because it had no further bearing on future outcomes.
2. The only one who had done well professionally was Tony, who had set up his own gardening business and was now busy enough to hire his brother to work with him. Interestingly enough, he was one of the men for whom imprisonment had become a normal fact of life, and though he described a transformational moment, in the rest of his interview he didn't present himself as having made a radical break with his past, except for in his offending behaviour. He did not use his legitimate and successful enterprise as a marker of a new identity.
3. Although see MacDonald et al. (2011), whose research suggests 'critical moments' of insight can be important in the desistance process.
4. http://www.sns.gov.uk/, accessed 21 March 2014.

Appendix II: Narrative Methods

1. For example, in the otherwise very sympathetic report of the Scottish Prisons Commission (2008), there is an implicit distinction made between short-term prisoners, who should not be incarcerated, and long-term prisoners 'whose crimes are serious and violent, and...who present a real risk to our safety' (p. 13).

Bibliography

Alpert, G. P. and Hicks, D. A. (1977). 'Prisoners' attitudes toward components of the legal and judicial systems', *Criminology*, 14(4): 461–482.

Apel, R., Blokland, A., Nieuwbeerta, P. and van Schellen, M. (2010). 'The impact of imprisonment on marriage and divorce: A risk set matching approach', *Journal of Quantitative Criminology*, 26(2): 269–300.

Applegate, B. K., Smith, H. P., Sitren, A. H. and Fariello Springer, N. (2009). 'From the inside: The meaning of probation to probationers', *Criminal Justice Review*, 34(1): 80–95.

Appleton, C. (2010). *Life After Life Imprisonment.* Oxford: Oxford University Press.

Aresti, A. (2010). *'Doing time after time': A hermeneutic phenomenological understanding of reformed ex-prisoners experiences of selfchange and identity negotiation.* (PhD). University of London, Birbeck.

Aresti, A., Eatough, V. and Brooks-Gordon, B. (2010). 'Doing time after time: An interpretative phenomenological analysis of reformed ex-prisoners' experiences of self-change, identity and career opportunities', *Psychology, Crime & Law*, 16(3): 169–190.

Armour, M., Rivaux, S. L. and Bell, H. (2009). 'Using context to build rigor application to two hermeneutic phenomenological studies', *Qualitative Social Work*, 8(1): 101–122.

Armstrong, S. and Weaver, B. (2010). *What Do the Punished Think of Punishment? The comparative experience of short prison sentences and community-based punishments* (Research Report No. 04/2010). SCCJR. Available at: http://www.sccjr. ac.uk/publications/what-do-the-punished-think-of-punishment-the-comparative-experience-of-short-term-prison-sentences-and-community-based-punishments/ Accessed 1 August 2012.

Ashkar, P. J. and Kenny, D. T. (2008). 'Views from the inside: Young offenders' subjective experiences of incarceration', *International Journal of Offender Therapy and Comparative Criminology*, 52(5): 584–597.

Atkinson, P. (1997). 'Narrative turn or blind alley?', *Qualitative Health Research*, 7(3): 325–344.

Banister, P., Burman, E., Parker, I., Taylor, M. and Tindall, C. (1994). *Qualitative Methods in Psychology: A Research Guide.* Buckingham: Open University Press.

Barry, M. (2006). 'Dispensing [with?] justice: Young people's views of the criminal justice system', in K. Gorman, M. Gregory, M. Hayles and N. Parton (eds), *Constructive Work with Offenders* (pp. 177–192). London: Jessica Kingsley.

Barry, M. (2007). 'Listening and learning: The reciprocal relationship between worker and client', *Probation Journal*, 54(4): 407–422.

Beetham, D. (1991). *The Legitimation of Power.* Basingstoke: Macmillan Education.

Berman, G. (2012). *Prison Population Statistics.* London: House of Commons Library. Available at: www.parliament.uk/briefing-papers/SN04334.pdf Accessed 25 October 2012.

Binswanger, I. A., Stern, M. F., Deyo, R. A., Heagerty, P. J., Cheadle, A., Elmore, J. G. and Koepsell, T. D. (2007). 'Release from prison – a high risk of death for former inmates', *New England Journal of Medicine*, 356(2): 157–165.

Birch, M. and Miller, T. (2000). 'Inviting intimacy: The interview as therapeutic opportunity', *International Journal of Social Research Methodology*, 3(3): 189–202.

Bird, S. M. and Hutchinson, S. J. (2003). 'Male drugs-related deaths in the fortnight after release from prison: Scotland, 1996–99', *Addiction*, 98(2): 185–190.

Blumstein, A. and Nakamura, K. (2009). 'Redemption in the presence of widespread criminal background checks', *Criminology*, 47(2): 327–359.

Boone, M. (2011). 'Judicial rehabilitation in the Netherlands: Balancing between safety and privacy', *European Journal of Probation*, 3(1): 63–78.

Bosworth, M. (1996). 'Resistance and compliance in women's prisons: Towards a critique of legitimacy', *Critical Criminology*, 7(2): 5–19.

Bottoms, A. (2001). 'Compliance and community penalties', in A. Bottoms, L. Gelsthorpe and S. Rex (eds), *Community Penalties: Change and Challenges* (pp. 87–116). Cullompton: Willan Publishing.

Bottoms, A. and Tankebe, J. (2012). 'Beyond procedural justice: A dialogic approach to legitimacy in criminal justice', *Journal of Criminal Law and Criminology*, 102(119): 101–150.

Bourdieu, P. (1999). *The Weight of the World: Social Suffering in Contemporary Society*. Cambridge: Polity Press.

Burnett, R. (2004). 'To reoffend or not to reoffend? The ambivalence of convicted property offenders', in S. Maruna and R. Immarigeon (eds), *After Crime and Punishment: Pathways to Offender Reintegration* (pp. 152–180). Cullompton: Willan Publishing.

Burnett, R. and Maruna, S. (2004). 'So "prison works", does it? The criminal careers of 130 men released from prison under Home Secretary, Michael Howard', *The Howard Journal of Criminal Justice*, 43(4): 390–404.

Burnett, R. and Maruna, S. (2006). 'The kindness of prisoners', *Criminology and Criminal Justice*, 6(1): 83–106.

Bushway, S. D. and Apel, R. (2012). 'A signaling perspective on employment-based reentry programming', *Criminology & Public Policy*, 11(1): 21–50.

Carlen, P. and Worrall, A. (2004). *Analysing Women's Imprisonment*. Cullompton: Willan Publishing.

Carrabine, E. (2004). *Power, Discourse and Resistance: A Genealogy of the Strangeways Prison Riot*. Aldershot: Ashgate.

Casper, J. D. (1972). *American Criminal Justice: The Defendant's Perspective*. Englewood Cliffs, NJ: Prentice Hall.

Casper, J. D. (1978). 'Having their day in court: Defendant evaluations of the fairness of their treatment', *Law & Society Review*, 12: 237–251.

Casper, J. D., Tyler, T. R. and Fisher, B. (1988). 'Procedural justice in felony cases', *Law & Society Review*, 22: 483–508.

Chase, S. (2005). 'Narrative enquiry: Multiple lenses, approaches, voices', in N. K. Denzin and Y. S. Lincoln (eds), *The SAGE Handbook of Qualitative Research*, 3rd edn, (pp. 651–679). Thousand Oaks, CA: SAGE.

Cheliotis, L. K. (2006). 'How iron is the iron cage of new penology? The role of human agency in the implementation of criminal justice policy', *Punishment & Society*, 8(3): 313–340.

Cohen, S. and Taylor, L. (1972). *Psychological Survival: The Experience of Long-Term Imprisonment*. Harmondsworth: Penguin.

Comfort, M. (2008). 'The best seven years I could'a done: The reconstruction of imprisonment as rehabilitation', in P. Carlen (ed.), *Imaginary Penalties* (pp. 252–274). Cullompton: Willan Publishing.

Commission on Women Offenders (2012). *Commission on Women Offenders*. Available at: http://www.scccj.org.uk/wp-content/uploads/2012/04/00391588_women_offenders_17thApril2012.pdf Accessed 28 June 2012.

Connell, R. (1996). 'Teaching the boys: New research on masculinity and gender strategies for schools', *The Teachers College Record*, 98(2): 206–235.

Council of Europe. (2003). *Recommendation on the management by prison administrations of life sentence and other long-term prisoners* (No. Recommendation (2003)23). Strasbourg: Council of Europe.

Crewe, B. (2006). 'Male prisoners' orientations towards female officers in an English prison', *Punishment & Society*, 8(4): 395–421.

Crewe, B. (2009). *The Prisoner Society: Power, Adaptation and Social Life in an English Prison*. Oxford: Oxford University Press.

Crowley, J. E. (2007). 'Friend or foe? Self-expansion, stigmatized groups and the researcher–participant relationship', *Journal of Contemporary Ethnography*, 36(6): 603–630.

Cullen, F. T. (1994). 'Social support as an organizing concept for criminology: Presidential address to the Academy of Criminal Justice Sciences', *Justice Quarterly*, 11(4): 527–559.

Curran, J., MacQueen, S. and Whyte, B. (2007). *"Forced to Make Amends": An Evaluation of the Community Reparation Order Pilots* (Research Publications). Edinburgh: Scottish Government. Available at: http://www.scotland.gov.uk/Publications/2007/08/21134602/0 Accessed 18 May 2009.

Dinwoodie, R. (2013, January 30). 'Call for inmates to have phones in cells', *Herald Scotland*. Available at: http://www.heraldscotland.com/politics/political-news/call-for-inmates-to-have-phones-in-cells.20049033 Accessed 1 April 2014.

Drago, F., Galbiati, R. and Vertova, P. (2009). 'The deterrent effects of prison: Evidence from a natural experiment', *Journal of Political Economy*, 117(2): 257–278.

Duff, R. A. (2001). *Punishment, Communication and Community*. Oxford: Oxford University Press.

Enosh, G. and Buchbinder, E. (2005). 'The interactive construction of narrative styles in sensitive interviews: The case of domestic violence research', *Qualitative Inquiry*, 11(4): 588–617.

Evans, T. and Wallace, P. (2008). 'A prison within a prison?', *Men and Masculinities*, 10(4): 484–507.

Ewald, A. and Uggen, C. (2012). 'The collateral effects of imprisonment on prisoners, their families and communities', in J. Petersilia and K. R. Reitz (eds), *The Oxford Handbook of Sentencing and Corrections* (pp. 83–103). Oxford University Press.

Ezzy, D. (2010). 'Qualitative interviewing as an embodied emotional performance', *Qualitative Inquiry*, 16(3): 163–170.

Fabiano, E. A., Robinson, D. and Porporino, F. J. (1991). *A Preliminary Assessment of the Cognitive Skills Training Program: A Component of Living Skills Programming* (Research Brief No. B-07). Ottawa, ON: Correctional Service of Canada.

Farrall, S. and Calverley, A. (2006). *Understanding Desistance From Crime.* Maidenhead: Open University Press.

Feeley, M. and Simon, J. (1992). 'The new penology: Notes on the emerging strategy of corrections and its implications', *Criminology*, 30(4): 449–474.

Flanagan, T. J. (1995). *Long-term Imprisonment: Policy, Science and Correctional Practice.* Thousand Oaks, CA: SAGE Publications. Available at: https://www.ncjrs.gov/App/abstractdb/AbstractDBDetails.aspx?id=154400 Accessed 12 February 2014.

Forste, R., Clarke, L. and Bahr, S. (2011). 'Staying out of trouble: Intentions of young male offenders', *International Journal of Offender Therapy and Comparative Criminology*, 55(3): 430–444.

Franke, D., Bierie, D. and Mackenzie, D. L. (2010). 'Legitimacy in corrections', *Criminology & Public Policy*, 9(1): 89–117.

Franzosi, R. (1998). 'Narrative analysis – or why (and how) sociologists should be interested in narrative', *Annual Review of Sociology*, 24(1): 517–554.

Garde, J. (2003). 'Masculinity and madness', *Counselling and Psychotheraphy Research*, 3(1): 6–15.

Garland, D. (1990). *Punishment and Modern Society: A Study in Social Theory.* Oxford: Clarendon.

Garland, D. (1992). 'Criminological knowledge and its relation to power. Foucault's geneology and criminology today', *British Journal of Criminology*, 32(4): 403–422.

Garland, D. (1996). 'The limits of the sovereign state: Strategies of crime control in comtemporary society', *British Journal of Criminology*, 36(4): 445–471.

Gergen, K. J. and Gergen, M. M. (1997). 'Narratives of the self', in L. P. Hinchman and S. K. Hinchman (eds), *Memory, Identity, Community: The Idea of Narrative in the Human Sciences* (pp. 161–184). Albany: State University of New York Press.

Giordano, P. C., Cernkovich, S. A. and Rudolph, J. L. (2002). 'Gender, crime and desistance: Toward a theory of cognitive transformation', *American Journal of Sociology*, 107(4): 990–1064.

Glassner, B. and Loughlin, J. (1987). *Drugs in Adolescent Worlds: Burnouts to Straights.* Basingstoke: Macmillan.

Goffman, E. (1959). *The Presentation of Self in Everyday Life.* New York: Penguin.

Goffman, E. (1968). *Asylums: Essays on the Social Situation of Mental Patients and Other Inmates.* Harmondsworth: Penguin Books.

Goffman, E. (1990). *Stigma: Notes on the Management of Spoiled Identity.* London: Penguin Books.

Habermas, T. and Bluck, S. (2000). 'Getting a life: The emergence of the life story in adolescence', *Psychological Bulletin*, 126(5): 748–769.

Hackett, S. and Scott, S. (2005). *Working together for children and young people with harmful sexual behaviours* (A Barnarno's Scotland Briefing). Ilford, Essex.

Halsey, M. (2007). 'On confinement: Resident and inmate perspectives of secure care and imprisonment', *Probation Journal*, 54(4): 338–367.

Hartwell, S., McMakin, R., Tansi, R. and Bartlett, N. (2010). '"I grew up too fast for my age": Postdischarge issues and experiences of male juvenile offenders', *Journal of Offender Rehabilitation*, 49(7): 495–515.

Harvey, J. (2005). 'Crossing the boundary: The transition of young adults into prison', in A. Liebling and S. Maruna (eds), *The Effects of Imprisonment* (pp. 232–254). Cullompton: Willan Publishing.

Herald Scotland (2013). 'MacAskill rules out phones in cells for prisoners', *Herald Scotland*, 27 February. Available at: http://www.heraldscotland.com/politics/political-news/macaskill-rules-out-phones-in-cells-for-prisoners.20355604 Accessed 1 April 2014.

Herzog-Evans, M. (2011a). 'Desisting in France: What probation officers know and do. A first approach', *European Probation Journal*, 3(2): 29–46.

Herzog-Evans, M. (2011b). 'Judicial rehabilitation in France: Helping with the desisting process and acknowledging achieved desistance', *European Journal of Probation*, 3(1): 4–19.

Hindley, C. B. (1979). 'Problems of interviewing in obtaining retrospective information', in L. Moss and H. Goldstein (eds), *The Recall Method in Social Surveys* (pp. 100–127). Windsor: University of London Institute of Education.

HM Chief Inspector of Prisons for Scotland (2009). *Annual Report 2008–2009* (Report). Edinburgh: Scottish Government. Available at: http://www.scotland.gov.uk/Publications/2009/05/05104027/7 Accessed 16 November 2010.

HM Inspectorate of Prisons (2010). *Report on HMP and YOI Cornton Vale*. Edinburgh: Scottish Government. Available at: http://www.scotland.gov.uk/Publications/2010/01/15135941/2 Accessed 14 March 2012.

Hockey, D. (2012). 'Analytical reflections on time in custody', *The Howard Journal of Criminal Justice*, 51(1): 67–78.

Hollway, W. and Jefferson, P. T. (2000). *Doing Qualitative Research Differently: Free Association, Narrative and the Interview Method*. London: SAGE.

Holstein, J. A. and Gubrium, J. F. (1997). 'Active interviewing', in D. Silverman (ed.), *Qualitative Research: Theory, Method and Practice* (pp. 140–161). London: SAGE.

Houchin, R. (2005). *Social Exclusion and Imprisonment in Scotland*. Edinburgh: Scottish Prison Service.

Hough, M., Jackson, J. and Bradford, B. (2013). 'Legitimacy, trust and compliance: An empirical test of procedural justice theory using the European Social Survey', in J. Tankebe and A. Liebling (eds), *Legitimacy and Criminal Justice: An International Exploration* (pp. 326–352). Oxford, UK: Oxford University Press.

Hutton, N. (1999). 'Sentencing in Scotland', in P. Duff and N. Hutton (eds), *Criminal Justice in Scotland* (pp. 166–181). Aldershot: Ashgate.

Hydén, M. (2008). 'Narrating sensitive topics', in M. Andrews, C. Squire and M. Tamboukou (eds), *Doing Narrative Research* (pp. 122–136). Thousand Oaks, CA: SAGE.

Indermaur, D. (1994). 'Offenders' perceptions of sentencing', *Australian Psychologist*, 29(2): 140–144.

Jackson, J., Bradford, B., Hough, M., Myhill, A., Quinton, P. and Tyler, T. R. (2012). 'Why do people comply with the law? Legitimacy and the influence of legal institutions', *British Journal of Criminology*, 52(6): 1051–1071.

Jackson, J., Tyler, T. R., Bradford, B., Taylor, D. and Shiner, M. (2010). 'Legitimacy and procedural justice in prisons', *Prison Service Journal*, 191: 4–10.

Jewkes, Y. (2005). 'Loss, liminality and the life sentence: Managing identity through a disrupted life course', in A. Liebling and S. Maruna (eds), *The Effects of Imprisonment* (pp. 366–388). Cullompton: Willan Publishing.

Josselson, R. (1995). 'Imagining the real. Empathy, narrative and the dialogic self', in R. Josselson and A. Lieblich (eds), *Interpreting Experience: The Narrative Study of Lives* (pp. 27–44). Thousand Oaks, CA: SAGE.

Justice Committee (2013). *Inquiry into Purposeful Activity in Prisons*. Edinburgh: Scottish Parliament. Available at: http://www.scottish.parliament.uk/parliamentarybusiness/CurrentCommittees/57752.aspx Accessed 1 April 2014.

Kolber, A. (2009). 'The Subjective Experience of Punishment', *Columbia Law Review*, 109: 182–236.

Kolstad, A. (1996). 'Imprisonment as rehabilitation: Offenders' assessment of why it does not work', *Journal of Criminal Justice*, 24(4): 323–335.

Kratcoski, P. and Scheijerman, K. (1974). 'Incarcerated male and female offenders' perceptions of their experiences in the criminal justice system', *Journal of Criminal Justice*, 2(1): 73–78.

Krohn, M. and Stratton, J. (1980). 'A sense of injustice – attitudes toward the criminal justice system and institutional adaptations', *Criminology*, 17: 495–504.

Kruttschnitt, C. and Gartner, R. (2005). *Marking Time in the Golden State: Women's Imprisonment in California*. Cambridge: Cambridge University Press.

Labov, W. (1972). *Language in the Inner City*. Philadelphia: University of Pennsylvania Press.

Labov, W. (2010). *Oral Narratives of Personal Experience*. Available at: http://www.ling.upenn.edu/~wlabov/ Accessed 23 June 2010.

Larson, C. J. and Berg, B. L. (1989). 'Inmates' perceptions of determinate and indeterminate sentences', *Behavioral Sciences & The Law*, 7(1): 127–137.

LeBel, T. P., Burnett, R., Maruna, S. and Bushway, S. (2008). 'The "chicken and egg" of subjective and social factors in desistance from crime', *European Journal of Criminology*, 5(2): 131–159.

Lieblich, A., Tuval-Mashiach, R. and Zilber, T. (1998). *Narrative Research: Reading, Analysis and Interpretation*. Thousand Oaks, CA: SAGE.

Liebling, A. (2004). *Prisons and Their Moral Performance: A Study of Values, Quality and Prison Life*. Clarendon Studies in Criminology. Oxford: Oxford University Press.

Liebling, A. (2011). 'Moral performance, inhuman and degrading treatment and prison pain', *Punishment & Society*, 13(5): 530–550.

Liebling, A., and Arnold, H. (2012). 'Social relationships between prisoners in a maximum security prison: violence, faith, and the declining nature of trust', *Journal of Criminal Justice* 40(5): 413–424.

Liebling, A. and Maruna, S. (2005). *The Effects of Imprisonment*. Cullompton: Willan Publishing.

Liebling, A., Arnold, H. and Straub, C. (2011). *An Exploration of Staff–Prisoner Relationships at HMP Whitemoor: Twelve Years On*. London: Home Office.

Lifers Public Safety Committee (2004). 'Ending the culture of street crime', *Prison Journal*, 84(4): 48–68.

Loucks, N. (2007). *Housing Needs of Prisoners and Ex-prisoners*. Glasgow: Robertson Trust. Available at: http://www.therobertsontrust.org.uk/index.php/download_file/-/view/75 Accessed 30 January 2012.

MacDonald, R., Webster, C., Shildrick, T. and Simpson, M. (2011). 'Paths of exclusion, inclusion and desistance', in S. Farrall, M. Hough, S. Maruna and R. Sparks (eds), *Escape Routes: Contemporary Perspectives on Life After Punishment* (pp. 134–157). New York: Routledge.

Maguire, M. (2000). 'Researching "street" criminals', in R.D. King and E. Wincup (eds), *Doing Research on Crime and Justice* (pp. 121–152). Oxford: Oxford University Press.

Maguire, M. and Raynor, P. (2006). 'How the resettlement of prisoners promotes desistance from crime', *Criminology and Criminal Justice*, 6(1): 19–38.

Maruna, S. (2001). *Making Good: How Ex-Convicts Reform and Rebuild Their Lives.* Washington, DC: American Psychological Association.

Maruna, S. (2011a). 'Judicial rehabilitation and the "Clean Bill of Health" in criminal justice', *European Journal of Probation*, 3(1): 97–117.

Maruna, S. (2011b). 'Reentry as a rite of passage', *Punishment & Society*, 13(1): 3–28.

Maruna, S. and Roy, K. (2007). 'Amputation or reconstruction? Notes on the concept of "knifing off" and desistance from crime', *Journal of Contemporary Criminal Justice*, 23(1): 104–124.

Maruna, S., Wilson, L. and Curran, K. (2006). 'Why God is often found behind bars: Prison conversions and the crisis of self-narrative', *Research in Human Development*, 3(2–3): 161–184.

Massoglia, M. (2008). 'Incarceration, health and racial disparities in health', *Law & Society Review*, 42(2): 275–306.

Mathiesen, T. (1965). *The Defences of the Weak.* London: Tavistock.

McAdams, D. P. (2001). 'The psychology of life stories', *Review of General Psychology*, 5(2): 100–122.

McAdams, D. P. (2008). 'Personal narratives and the life story', in O. P. John, R. W. Robins and L. A. Pervin (eds), *Handbook of Personality: Theory and Research*, 3rd edn, (pp. 242–262). New York: Guildford Press.

McConnell, C. (2013, November 19). *A Golden Era for the Scottish Prison Service Helping to Build a Safer Scotland – Unlocking Potential –Transforming Lives.* Presented at the Scottish Prison Service Conference, Edinburgh. Available at http://www.sps.gov.uk/nmsruntime/saveasdialog.aspx?lID=2127&sID=1395 Accessed 10 December 2013.

McCorkle, L. W. and Korn, R. (1954). 'Resocialization within walls', *The ANNALS of the American Academy of Political and Social Science*, 293(1): 88–98.

McGinnis, J. H. and Carlson, K. A. (1981). 'Offenders' perceptions of their sentences', *Journal of Offender Counselling, Services and Rehabilitation*, 5(34): 27–37.

McKendy, J. P. (2006). 'I'm very careful about that: Narrative and agency of men in prison', *Discourse Society*, 17(4): 473–502.

McNeill, F. (2006). 'A desistance paradigm for offender management', *Criminology and Criminal Justice*, 6(1): 39–62.

McNeill, F. (2012). 'Four forms of "offender" rehabilitation: Towards an interdisciplinary perspective', *Legal and Criminological Psychology*, 17(1): 18–36.

McNeill, F. (2013). 'When punishment is rehabilitation', in G. Bruinsma and D. Weisburd (eds), *Encyclopedia of Criminology and Criminal Justice*. New York: Springer Verlag.

McQuillan, M. (2000). *The Narrative Reader.* London: Routledge.

McWilliams, W. and Pease, K. (1990). 'Probation practice and an end to punishment', *The Howard Journal of Criminal Justice*, 29(1): 14–24.

Merton, R. K. (1938). 'Social structure and anomie', *American Sociological Review*, 3(5): 672–682.

Michaels, S. (1981). '"Sharing time": Children's narrative styles and differential access to literacy', *Language in Society*, 10(03): 423–442.

Michaels, S. and Cazden, C. B. (1984). 'Teacher/child collaboration as oral preparation for literacy', in B. B. Schieffelin (ed.), *The Acquisition of Literacy: Ethnographic Perspectives* (pp. 132–154). Norwood, NJ: Ablex.

Miller, D. L. (2011). 'Being called to account: Understanding adolescents' narrative identity construction in institutional contexts', *Qualitative Social Work*, 10(3): 311–328.

Miller, J. and Glassner, B. (1997). 'The "inside" and the "outside". Finding realities in interviews', in D. Silverman (ed.), *Qualitative Research: Theory, Method and Practice* (pp. 125–139). London: SAGE.

Mills, A. and Codd, H. (2008). 'Prisoners' families and offender management: Mobilizing social capital', *Probation Journal*, 55(1): 9–24.

Moffitt, T. E. (1993). 'Adolescence-limited and life-course-persistent antisocial behavior: A developmental taxonomy', *Psychological Review*, 100: 674–701.

Mooney, G., Croall, H. and Munro, M. (2010). 'Social inequalities, criminal justice and social control', in H. Croall, G. Mooney and M. Munro (eds), *Criminal Justice in Scotland* (pp. 21–42). Cullompton: Willan Publishing.

Morgenstern, C. (2011). 'Judicial rehabilitation in Germany – the use of criminal records and the removal of recorded convictions', *European Journal of Probation*, 3(1): 20–35.

Munro, M. (2010, March 9). Parliamentary Report for 1–5 March, 2010. *C J Scotland*. Available at: http://www.cjscotland.co.uk/2010/03/parliamentary-report-for-the-1st-5th-march-2010/ Accessed 29 November 2011.

Murray, J. (2005). 'The effects of imprisonment on families and children of prisoners', in A. Liebling and S. Maruna (eds), *The Effects of Imprisonment* (pp. 442–462). Cullompton: Willan Publishing.

Murray, J. (2007). 'The cycle of punishment: Social exclusion of prisoners and their children', *Criminology and Criminal Justice*, 7(1): 55–81.

Murray, J. and Farrington, D. P. (2008). 'Parental imprisonment: Long-lasting effects on boys' internalizing problems through the life course', *Development and Psychopathology*, 20(01): 273–290.

Nagin, D. S., Cullen, F. T. and Jonson, C. L. (2009). 'Imprisonment and reoffending', *Crime & Justice*, 38: 115–413.

Nicholson, C. G. B. (1981). *The Law and Practice of Sentencing in Scotland*. Edinburgh: W. Green.

Norrick, N. R. (2005). 'The dark side of tellability', *Narrative Inquiry*, 15(2): 323–343.

Pager, D. (2003). 'The mark of a criminal record', *American Journal of Sociology*, 108(5): 937–975.

Pasupathi, M. and Rich, B. (2005). 'Inattentive listening undermines self-verification in personal storytelling', *Journal of Personality*, 73(4): 1051–1086.

Patrick, S. and Marsh, R. (2001). 'Perceptions of punishment and rehabilitation among inmates in a medium security prison: A consumers' report', *Journal of Offender Rehabilitation*, 33(3): 47–64.

Pavlenko, A. (2002). 'Narrative study: Whose story is it, anyway?', *TESOL Quarterly*, 36(2): 213–218.

Petersilia, J. (2000). 'When prisoners return to the community: Political, economic and social consequences', *Sentencing and Corrections*, 9: 1–7.

Pew Center on the States (2012). *Time Served: The High Cost, Low Return of Longer Prison Terms*. Washington, DC: The Pew Charitable Trusts. Available at: http://www.pewstates.org/research/reports/time-served-85899394616 Accessed 12 February 2014.

Piquero, A. R. (2004). 'Somewhere between persistence and desistance: The intermittency of criminal careers', in S. Maruna and R. Immarigeon (eds), *After Crime* and Punishment: Pathways to Offender Reintegration (pp. 102–125). Cullompton: Willan Publishing.

Polanyi, L. (1985). *Telling the American Story: A Structural and Cultural Analysis of Conversational Storytelling*. Norwood, NJ: Ablex.

Polkinghorne, D. E. (2007). 'Validity issues in narrative research', *Qualitative Inquiry*, 13(4): 471–486.

Pollack, W. S. (1995). 'Deconstructing dis-identification: Rethinking psychoanalytic concepts of male development', *Psychoanalysis & Psychotherapy*, 12(1): 30–45.

Presser, L. (2008). *Been a Heavy Life: Stories of Violent Men*. Urbana, IL: University of Illinois Press.

Presser, L. (2009). 'The narratives of offenders', *Theoretical Criminology*, 13(2): 177–200.

Rex, S. (2005). *Reforming Community Penalties*. Cullompton: Willan Publishing.

Riessman, C. K. (1997). 'A short story about long stories', *Journal of Narrative and Life History*, 7: 155–158.

Riessman, C. K. (2002). 'Analysis of personal narratives', in J. F. Gubrium and J. A. Holstein (eds), *Handbook of Interview Research: Context & Method* (pp. 695–710). Thousand Oaks, CA: SAGE.

Riessman, C. K. (2003). 'Performing identities in illness narrative: Masculinity and multiple sclerosis', *Qualitative Research*, 3(1): 5–33.

Riessman, C. K. (2008). *Narrative Methods for the Human Sciences*. Thousand Oaks, CA: SAGE.

Riessman, C. K. and Quinney, L. (2005). 'Narrative in social work: A critical review', *Qualitative Social Work*, 4(4): 391–412.

Rijksen, R. (1958). *Meningen van Gedetineerden over de Strafrechtspleging*. Assen: Van Gorcum.

Ritchie, J., Lewis, J. and Elam, G. (2003). 'Designing and selecting samples', in J. Ritchie and J. Lewis (eds), *Qualitative Research Practice: A Guide for Social Science Students and Researchers* (pp. 77–108). London: SAGE.

Robinson, G. (2008). 'Late-modern rehabilitation: The evolution of a penal strategy', *Punishment & Society*, 10(4): 429–445.

Robinson, G. and McNeill, F. (2008). 'Exploring the dynamics of compliance with community penalties', *Theoretical Criminology*, 12(4): 431–449.

Ruspini, E. (2000). *Longitudinal Research in the Social Sciences*. Social Research Update, 28. Available at: http://sru.soc.surrey.ac.uk/SRU28.html Accessed 13 July 2010.

Sabo, D. F., Kupers, T. A. and London, W. J. (2001). *Prison Masculinities*. Philadelphia: Temple University Press.

Sampson, R. J. and Laub, J. H. (2003). 'Life-course desisters? Trajectories of crime among delinquent boys followed to age 70', *Criminology*, 41(3): 555–592.

Sampson, R. J. and Laub, J. H. (2005). 'A life-course view of the development of crime', *The ANNALS of the American Academy of Political and Social Science*, 602(1): 12–45.

Schinkel, M. (in press-a). 'Punishment as moral communication: the experiences of long-term prisoners', *Punishment & Society*.

Schinkel, M. (in press-b). 'Adaptation, the meaning of imprisonment and outcomes after release – the impact of the prison regime', *Prison Service Journal*.

Schinkel, M. and Whyte, B. (2009). *Formative Evaluation of the Constructs PSSO Groupwork Programme* (Briefing Paper No. 7). Towards Effective Practice.

Edinburgh: Criminal Justice Social Work Development Centre for Scotland. Available at: http://www.cjsw.ac.uk/cjsw/files/TEP7.pdf Accessed 30 September 2009.

Schinkel, M., Jardine, C., Curran, J., Whyte, B. and Nugent, B. (2009). *Final Report of the Evaluation of the Routes Out Of Prison Project*. Edinburgh: Criminal Justice Social Work Development Centre for Scotland.

Schneider, A. and McKim, W. (2003). 'Stigmatization among probationers', *Journal of Offender Rehabilitation*, 38(1): 19–31.

Schnittker, J. and John, A. (2007). 'Enduring stigma: The long-term effects of incarceration on health', *Journal of Health and Social Behavior*, 48(2): 115–130.

Scottish Government (2007). *Reforming and Revitalising: Report of the Review of Community Penalties*. Edinburgh: Scottish Government. Available at: http://www.scotland.gov.uk/Publications/2007/11/20142739/8 Accessed 6 November 2008.

Scottish Government (2008). *Sentencing Guidelines and a Scottish Sentencing Council: Consultation and Proposals* (Consultation). Available at: http://www.scotland.gov.uk/Publications/2008/08/29100017/0 Accessed 24 November 2010.

Scottish Government (2009). *Statistical Bulletin: Crime and Justice Series: Prison Statistics Scotland: 2008–09*. Edinburgh: Scottish Government. Available at: http://www.scotland.gov.uk/Publications/2009/11/27092125/4 Accessed 16 November 2010.

Scottish Government (2012a). *Prison Statistics and Population Projections Scotland: 2011–12* (Statistics Publication). Edinburgh: Scottish Government. Available at: http://www.scotland.gov.uk/Publications/2012/06/6972/3 Accessed 7 December 2012.

Scottish Government (2012b). *Income and Poverty – Main Analysis*. Available at: http://www.scotland.gov.uk/Topics/Statistics/Browse/Social-Welfare/IncomePoverty/CoreAnalysis Accessed 31 October 2012.

Scottish Prisons Commission (2008). *Scotland's Choice: Report of The Scottish Prisons Commission*. Edinburgh: Scottish Prisons Commission. Available at: http://www.scotland.gov.uk/Publications/2008/06/30162955/0 Accessed 6 November 2008.

Scottish Prison Service (2011). *Scottish Prison Service Delivery Plan 2011/12*. Scottish Prison Service. Available at: http://www.sps.gov.uk/Publications/Publication-3115.aspx Accessed 13 January 2012.

Scottish Prison Service (2012). *Annual Report and Accounts 2011–2012*. Edinburgh: Scottish Prison Service.

Scottish Prison Service (2013). *Unlocking Potential, Transforming Lives: Summary Report of the Scottish Prison Service Organisational Review*. Edinburgh: Scottish Prison Service. Available at: http://www.sps.gov.uk/nmsruntime/saveasdialog.aspx?lID=2118&sID=13 Accessed 12 February 2014.

Searle, W., Knaggs, T. and Simonsen, K. (2003). *Talking About Sentences and Crime: The Views of People on Periodic Detention*. Wellington, New Zealand: Ministry of Justice. Available at: http://www.justice.govt.nz/publications/publications-archived/2003/talking-about-sentences Accessed 20 February 2009.

Sexton, L. (2012). *Under the Penal Gaze: An Empirical Examination of Penal Consciousness Among Prison Inmates*. (PhD). University of California, Irvine.

Shapland, J. and Bottoms, A. (2011). 'Reflections on social values, offending and desistance among young adult recidivists', *Punishment & Society*, 13(3): 256–282.

Sherman, L. W. (1993). 'Defiance, deterrence and irrelevance: A theory of the criminal sanction', *Journal of Research in Crime and Delinquency*, 30(4): 445–473.

Silverman, D. (2001). *Interpreting Qualitative Data: Methods for Analyzing Talk, Text and Interaction*. London: SAGE.

Singer, J. A. (2004). 'Narrative identity and meaning making across the adult lifespan: An introduction', *Journal of Personality*, 72(3): 437–460.

Smith, D. J. (2007). 'The foundations of legitimacy', in T. R. Tyler (ed.), *Legitimacy and Criminal Justice: International Perspectives* (pp. 30–58). New York: Russell Sage Foundation.

Social Exclusion Unit (2002). *Reducing Re-Offending by Ex-Prisoners*. London: Social Exclusion Unit. Available at: https://www.prisonersfamilies.org.uk/uploadedFiles/2010_Policy/reducing%20reoffending%20by%20ex-prisoners%202002.pdf Accessed 19 July 2012.

Soothill, K. and Francis, B. (2009). 'When do ex-offenders become like non-offenders?', *The Howard Journal of Criminal Justice*, 48(4): 373–387.

Sparks, R. and Bottoms, A. (1995). 'Legitimacy and order in prisons', *The British Journal of Sociology*, 46(1): 45–62.

Sparks, R., Bottoms, A. and Hay, W. (1996). *Prisons and the Problem of Order*. Clarendon Studies in Criminology. Oxford: Clarendon Press.

Stanley, L. and Temple, B. (2008). 'Narrative methodologies: Subjects, silences, re-readings and analyses', *Qualitative Research*, 8(3): 275–281.

Sunshine, J. and Tyler, T. R. (2003). 'The role of procedural justice and legitimacy in shaping public support for policing', *Law & Society*, 37(3): 513–548.

Sykes, G. (1958). *The Society of Captives*. Princeton: Princeton University Press.

Sykes, G. and Matza, D. (1957). 'Techniques of neutralization: A theory of delinquency', *American Sociological Review*, 22(6): 664–670.

Tankebe, J. and Liebling, A. (eds). (2013). *Legitimacy and Criminal Justice: An International Exploration*. Oxford, UK: Oxford University Press.

Taxman, F., Young, D. and Byrne, J. (2004). 'With eyes wide open: Formalizing community and social control intervention in offender reintegration programs', in S. Maruna and R. Immarigeon (eds), *After Crime and Punishment: Pathways to Offender Reintegration* (pp. 233–260). Cullompton: Willan Publishing.

Tunnell, K. D. (1992). *Choosing Crime: The Criminal Calculus of Property Offenders*. Chicago, IL: Nelson-Hall.

Tyler, T. R. (1990). *Why People Obey the Law: Procedural Justice, Legitimacy and Compliance*. New Haven, CT: Yale University Press.

Tyler, T. R. (1997). *Social Justice in a Diverse Society*. Boulder, CO: Westview Press.

Tyler, T. R. (2003). 'Procedural justice, legitimacy and the effective rule of law', *Crime & Justice*, 30: 283–357.

Tyler, T. R. (2006). 'Restorative justice and procedural justice: Dealing with rule breaking', *Journal of Social Issues*, 62(2): 307–326.

Tyler, T. R. (2010). 'Legitimacy in corrections', *Criminology & Public Policy*, 9(1): 127–134.

Vaughan, B. (2007). 'The internal narrative of desistance', *British Journal of Criminology*, 47(3): 390–404.

Vincent, N. (2006). *Self-made Man: My Year Disguised as a Man*. London: Atlantic Books.

Walters, G. D. (1990). *The Criminal Lifestyle: Patterns of Serious Criminal Conduct*. Thousand Oaks, CA: SAGE.

Wang, Q. and Conway, M. A. (2004). 'The stories we keep: Autobiographical memory in American and Chinese middle-aged adults', *Journal of Personality*, 72(5): 911–938.

Ward, Tony and Marshall, B. (2007). 'Narrative identity and offender rehabilitation', *International Journal of Offender Therapy and Comparative Criminology*, 51(3): 279–297.

Ward, Tony and Maruna, S. (2007). *Rehabilitation: Beyond the Risk Paradigm*. London: Routledge.

Watson, D. (1996). 'Individuals and institutions: The case of work and employment', in M. Wetherell (ed.), *Identities, Groups and Social Issues* (pp. 239–298). London: SAGE Publications.

Weaver, B. and Armstrong, S. (2011). *User Views of Punishment. The dynamics of community-based punishment: Insider views from the outside*. (Research Report No. 03/11). SCCJR. Available at: http://www.sccjr.ac.uk/documents/Report%20 2011%2003%20User%20Views%20of%20Punishment-1.pdf Accessed 1 August, 2012.

Wheeler, S. (1961). 'Socialization in correctional communities', *American Sociological Review*, 26(5): 697–712.

Wilkinson, R. G. and Pickett, K. (2010). *The Spirit Level: Why More Equal Societies Almost Always Do Better*. London: Penguin.

Wood, J., Williams, G. R. and James, M. (2010). 'Incapacitation and imprisonment: Prisoners' involvement in community-based crime', *Psychology, Crime & Law*, 16(7): 601–615.

Index

accommodation, 45–7, 102, 120
adaptation
  to life outside 80–8
  to prison, 24, 51, 54–5, 61, 71–7,
    122, 130–1
Alan, 7, 9, 31, 33, 38, 64–5, 101, 124
Alex, 7, 44, 45, 51, 55, 67–8, 71, 72,
    76, 92, 102, 135–6
Andy, 7, 32, 39, 41–2, 44, 54, 65, 84,
    86, 104, 106, 107–8, 109, 142
anger, 22, 88, 92
appealing the sentence, 76, 136
'as if' reform, 40–2, 44, 124

children, 5, 6, 43, 59, 73, 74, 130, 131,
    136, 137, 140–1, 143
Chris, 7, 33, 39, 43, 58–9, 66, 135
circumscribed horizons, 51, 73–5, 80,
    104, 122, 123, 125, 129, 130–1
cognitive behavioural courses, 31–6,
    38, 44, 47, 69, 97, 120, 125, 128
Colin, 7, 37, 44, 57, 58, 96–101, 136
compliance, 34, 92–4, 120
confrontation, 42, 43
consistency (in sentencing and prison
    rules), 15, 21, 22, 26, 55, 62, 63,
    64, 65, 91, 122, 123, 12, 161n4.3
coping-acceptance, 68–72, 84–5, 93,
    123
coping strategies, 72–5
criminal justice
  fairness of process, see procedural
    justice
  system, 32, 67, 78–9, 91, 92, 124,
    125, 129, 161n3
Criminal Justice and Licensing
    (Scotland) Act, 9–10
criminal justice social workers, 5, 87,
    111, 120, 126
criminal punishment
  see also imprisonment; prison
    sentences
  interpretations of, 1–2

justifications for, 3–5, 28–9,
    58
meaning of, 119–21
prisoner perceptions of, 13–27,
    see also long-term prisoners:
    perceptions of, about sentence;
    long-term prisoners: perceptions
    of, on punishment
purpose of, perceptions about,
    13–17
criminal records, 107, 109, 117, 122,
    133–4

Dan, 7, 30, 34, 40–1, 43, 53, 76, 102,
    137
David, 7, 9, 29, 30–1, 56, 101
deprivation, 11–12, 14, 36, 38, 117,
    153
desistance, 2–3, 43, 46, 61, 96–7,
    99–104, 109–18, 123–4, 133
deterrence, 3, 4, 14, 26, 28, 49–56, 61,
    120, 121
Devan, 7, 30, 78–9, 101, 121, 124,
    137–8, 155–6
diachronic self-control, 106, 121
distributive justice, 19–20
Doug, 7, 32, 45, 46, 63, 73, 74, 75, 96,
    98–9, 100, 101, 121, 138
drug use, see substance abuse
dull compulsion, 75–7, 90–1, 92

education, 14, 40, 48
employment 4, 47–9, 82, 106–10,
    113, 117–18, 120, 122, 133–4

fairness, 17–23, 26, 64–5, 90, 122–5,
    see also legitimacy
family and friends, 73–5, 102, 103,
    125, 128, 131, see also children
female prisoners, 5, 128, 130

general guilt, 68, 69, 84, 91, 93, 122,
    123

Gordon, 7, 29, 31, 34, 44, 58, 63,
    67–8, 69, 92, 97, 99, 100, 101,
    103, 139
Graham, 7, 30, 34–6, 45, 69, 73, 99,
    139–49, 157
group discourse, *see* prisoner group
    discourse
guilt, 17, 63, 67–8, 84, 89, 91, 103,
    122, 123, 136, 139

health (mental and physical), 4, 5, 47,
    106, 110, 142, 143
housing, *see* accommodation

Ian, 7, 37, 39, 46, 47, 59, 64, 73, 74,
    77, 140, 156
identity, 75, 78, 95, 97, 101, 103,
    107–8, 111–12, 113, 114, 115–18,
    123–5, 130, 133, 147, 149–51,
    162n2
  non-offender identity, 78, 95, 115,
    124, 157
  non-starters, 101, 102, 103
  illegitimacy, *see* legitimacy
imprisonment
  acceptance of, 68–72, 75–7, 84–94
  adaptation to, 24, 51, 54–5, 61,
    71–7, 130–1
  cost of, 1
  experience of, 2–3, 23–5, 128–9
  impact of, 3, 71–7, 80–8
  inequality and, 11–12
  inevitability of, 76–7
  long-term, 10, 23–5
  meaning of, 5–9, 15–16, 28–61
  non-acceptance of, 77–80, 87–8
  short-term, 5, 11, 22, 40, 51, 130
  stigma of, 4, 5, 109, 117, 122, 129,
    134
  transformation through, 96–104,
    112–16
  unintended meanings and
    consequences of, 4–5, 121–2, 133
  as warehousing, 5, 9, 40
incapacitation, 3, 4, 14, 28, 57–8, 60
incentive schemes, 25, *see also*
    progression through prison
    regime
individual counseling, 131–2

inequality, 11–12
injustice, 26, 47, 63, 67, 68, 78, 88
inmates, *see* long-term prisoners;
    prisoners
institutionalisation, 51–2, 54, 61, 79,
    80, 82–4, 126
isolation, 40, 80–1, 104–5, 121, 127

Jack, 7, 43–4, 47–8, 49, 50, 51, 52, 66,
    77, 81, 83, 105, 107, 109–10, 143
James, 7, 36, 40, 41, 44, 66, 69, 70, 72,
    75, 92, 97, 99–101, 141
judge, 17, 50, 56, 58–9, 66, 70, 78, 84,
    87, 125
judicial rehabilitation, 132–4
just deserts, 3, 4, 18, 19, 20, 56, 66
justice, 17, 18
  distributive, 19–20
  procedural, 18–20, 46–7, 67,
    161n4.2

legitimacy, 19–20, 23, 25, 62, 68,
    80–8, 90–2, 94, 124
liberty, loss of, 56–7
licence, 11, 16, 17, 46, 47, 77, 80–8,
    104–10, 114–15, 120, 133
  see also release
life-sentenced prisoners, 78
Lino, 7, 32, 33–4, 43, 49–50, 59, 80–1,
    83, 85, 105, 106, 109, 110, 143–4
long-term prisoners
  narratives of, 1, 6, 9
  perceptions of, about sentence, 2, 3,
    5–6, 28–61
  perceptions of, on punishment,
    13–27
  prison regimes and, 129
  research on, 5–9
  in Scotland, 10–11

Malcolm, 7, 9, 36, 50, 63
managerialism, 29, 37–40, 60, 120
Mark, 7, 37, 84, 103–4, 106
masculinity, 16, 53–4, 61, 121
Mohammed, 7, 32, 44, 48, 73–4, 81,
    84, 86, 107, 144
morality, 14, 17, 19, 25, 26, 45, 64, 65,
    88, 92, 93, 124, 161n2
'moral' prisons, 2, 23, 130

narrative, 95–104, 110–16, 124–5
  defined, 147–8
  demands of, 96–104
  impact of audience, 155–60
  influences on, 152–3, 154
  narrative analysis, 153–4
  narrative methods, 6, 146–60
  role of, 148–52
  social distance, 156–7
narrative vignettes, 135–45
Neil, 7, 44, 52, 56, 66, 71–2, 74, 103,
  156–7
New Penology, 120, 147

open estate, 33, 34, 43, 46–7, 120,
  139, 145

Paul, 7, 9, 31, 39, 55, 101
parole, see license
parole officers, *see* criminal justice
  social workers
personal change, 43–5, 60, 61, 79, 86,
  99, 103, 111–12
  see also transformation;
  transformation narratives
Peter, 7, 42, 44, 66–7, 71, 72, 78–80,
  83, 100, 101, 103, 112, 123, 141,
  151
police, 17, 26, 67, 105
poverty, *see* deprivation
powerlessness, 46–7, 74, 89, 90, 110
power/power relations, 23, 24, 25,
  75–6, 82–3, 91, 92
prison environment, impact of, 71–7,
  80–8, 129–30
prisoner group discourse, 35, 40, 54,
  125, 126, 153
prisoners
  relationships between, 23, 42, 157
  staff relationships with, 11, 13–14,
  23, 24, 25, 26, 60, 107, 129
prisonisation, 82–3
prison regimes, 23, 24, 62, 91, 120,
  125, 128–30
prisons
  adaptation to, 24, 51, 54–5, 61,
  71–7, 122, 130–1
  conditions in, 26, 50–4, 57, 75, 76,
  128–30

Scottish, 11
  subcultures in, 23, 82–3, *see also*
  prisoner group discourse
prison sentences
  see also criminal punishment;
  imprisonment
  acceptance of, 68–72, 75–7, 84–94,
  122–3
  end of, 77
  evaluation of, 62–8
  expectations about, 63–4, 122
  fairness of, 17–23, 26, 90, 122–5
  inconsistency in, 63–4
  long-term, 10, 23–5
  meanings ascribed to, 125–7
  opposition, 25, 26, 58, 68, 69, 71,
  72, 75, 124, 127
  perception of, 1–3, 5–6, 13–27,
  28–61
  purposes of, perceived, 28–61
probation, 5, 14, 16–17
procedural justice, 18–20, 46–7, 67,
  161n4.2
Proceeds of Crime Act, 64–5
progression through prison regime,
  33–4, 46–7, 120
proportionality, 91
punishment, 55–7
  see also criminal punishment
punitive purpose, 15–16, 55–7
purpose, of punishment, 13–17, 28–61

redemption scripts, 110–12, 114–15
reflection/time to think, 40–1
reform, 3, 4, 14, 29, 30–45, 60, 120
  see also rehabilitation
  achievement of, 43–5
  'as if', 40–2, 44, 124
  cognitive behavioural courses and,
  31–6, 38
  individual approaches vs.
  managerialism, 37–40
reform narratives, 97–104, *see also*
  transformation narratives
regime dimensions, 23, 24, 62, 91,
  120, 125, 128–30
rehabilitation, 3, 4, 13–16, 25–30,
  45–9, 60, 120, 128
  see also reform

rehabilitation – *continued*
  concept of, 45
  drug-related, 47–8
  individual, 131–2
  judicial, 132–4
release, 11, 45, *see also* licence
  problems after, 45–9, 51–2, 54, 61,
    79, 80–81, 82–4, 102, 104–10,
    113–14, 118–19, 120, 121, 122,
    126, 127, 133–4
  preparation for, 47
resources on the outside, 101–3, 111,
  114, 116, 123, 124, 125
responsibility, 3, 36, 83, 111, 121, 137,
  153
retribution, 3, 4, 14, 28, 55–7, 60
risk assessment, 38
Robert, 7, 30, 47, 65, 101, 161n3.1
role dispossession, 83, *see also*
  institutionalisation
routines, 26, 75–7, 81–2, 83, 93, 118,
  121, 131

Scotland
  Gini coefficient, 11
  imprisonment in, 9–10
  prisons in, 11
Scottish Prison Service, 10, 40, 47

self-perception, *see* identity
short-term imprisonment, 5, 11, 22,
  40, 51, 130
Smitty, 8, 44, 50–1, 53, 64, 67, 84,
  89–90, 104, 105
staff-prisoner relationships, 11, 13–14,
  23, 24, 25, 26, 60, 107, 129
Stephen, 8, 38, 45, 48, 57, 65, 83,
  87–8
stigma, 4, 5, 109, 117, 122, 129, 134
study participants, characteristics of,
  7–8
substance abuse, 5, 43, 47–8
surveillance, 105–6

Tim, 8, 43, 53, 54, 59, 80, 81, 83, 84,
  86
Tony, 8, 43–4, 48, 52, 77, 82, 83, 105,
  144–5, 162n2
transformation, 96–104, 124–5, 133
transformation narratives, 97–104,
  110–16, 124–5

unemployment, 5, 110, 118, 122, *see
  also* employment

Whitemoor prison, 25, 129–30
work, *see* employment

Printed and bound by CPI Group (UK) Ltd, Croydon, CR0 4YY